PIONEERS OF BASEBALL

BROWN BROTHERS

"The One and Only" — Babe Ruth in action

PIONEERS OF BASEBALL

by Robert Smith

BOSTON LITTLE, BROWN AND COMPANY TORONTO

FIRST EDITION

T 04/78

Library of Congress Cataloging in Publication Data

Smith, Robert, 1905–
Pioneers of baseball.

CONTENTS: Alexander Joy Cartwright, real father of the game. — William Henry (Harry) Wright, father of professional baseball. — Albert Goodwill (A.G.) Spalding, father of the National League. [etc.]
1. Baseball players — United States — Biography — Juvenile literature. 2. Baseball — United States — History — Juvenile literature. [1. Baseball players. 2. Baseball — History] I. Title.
GV865.A1S583 796.357'092'2 [B] [920] 77-18820
ISBN 0-316-80156-9

Published simultaneously in Canada
by Little, Brown & Company (Canada) Limited

PRINTED IN THE UNITED STATES OF AMERICA

for my young cousin
Mike Turner

CONTENTS

PIONEERS OF BASEBALL

NATIONAL BASEBALL HALL OF FAME

Alexander Cartwright

ALEXANDER JOY CARTWRIGHT

Real Father of the Game

The men who run professional baseball persist, for reasons you and I will never understand, in naming Abner Doubleday as the inventor of baseball. This is not much further from the truth than saying that the game was invented by Henry Ford or King George III. Abner Doubleday's claim is based entirely on a letter written by a very old man who went to school with him and who recalled, or thought he recalled, that one day in 1839 Abner showed his friends how to play a game with a ball and bases. But the game the old man described was a game that had been played for at least a century in this land; there were no competing sides (just the batter against the whole school yard full of playmates), there were no innings, posts were used for bases, and a runner could be put out by hitting him with the ball as he ran from one post to another.

This elementary form of the game was known by different names in different parts of the country. It was often called *town ball,* because it involved all the young men in town when played on town meeting day.

Or it was known as *round ball,* because it had obviously been derived from the ancient British game of rounders. Or it was named *sting ball, soak ball,* or *burn ball,* because of its most interesting feature — belting a runner with the ball, sometimes from close up, as he sought the safety of a post or base.

But there was another kind of ball played in the eastern cities in the early 1800s (and probably for many years before that). This was a game that faintly resembled cricket, in that, in some forms, it involved running back and forth between bases while the ball was being retrieved and called for grounding the bat in a *hole* (or *crease*) to attain safety from being put out. The young folk who were playing this game when the nation itself was young called the game *catapult ball,* because it did not require the services of a pitcher, or *bowler.* Instead, the flat bat would be laid seesaw fashion across a log or rock, with the ball set on the lower end. Then one player would hit the upper end of the bat with his fist or foot to send the ball up in the air for the *striker* to hit with his hand.

Even when youngsters began to pitch (or *bowl*) the ball to the batter, the game was still called catapult ball, or just *cat ball.* And when it was played, as it often was, with just one batter and one hole, it was called *one-hole cat.*

Both round ball and one-hole cat, along with some other versions of the game, were played and enjoyed in vacant lots throughout New York City in the 1840s. One group of young men who lived on Murray Hill (around Thirty-fourth Street) in New York used to gather every Sunday on a lot near the present corner of Thirty-fourth Street and Lexington Avenue to play one or another form of baseball — the choice of which form depended on how many players showed up. It was on this lot that the true ancestor of modern baseball, the game called the *New York game,* or the *Knickerbocker game,* was first laid out and played. And the man who worked it out was an extraordinarily tall young fellow named Alexander Cartwright.

Cartwright stood head and shoulders over most of his playmates: he was six-foot-two in the days when a six-footer was deemed a giant. Because he was both tall and inordinately strong and agile, he was the natural leader of the crowd. When he showed up at the playground with a design for a new ball game worked out on paper, his mates all hastened to join his experiment. They had no measuring instruments, so the distances were given in paces — forty-two paces from base to base, very close to the present ninety feet. The bases formed a square, but actually they were meant to be four points on a circle, with the home base opposite the second base and the first base opposite the third. This form of *base circle,* as it was called, was already being used in a Philadelphia form of the game, except that the bases were much closer together — too close, by Cartwright's standards. But what the polite young men from Murray Hill liked best about the game was that Cartwright had taken the rowdyism out of it by making it possible to put a runner out by getting the ball to the base ahead of him or by tagging him with the ball, instead of hitting him with it. These lads, all dressed in clean flannel for Sunday, preferred a game with no violence in it. (And when they finally formed themselves into the Knickerbocker Base Ball Club to play match games with other gentlemen's clubs in town, they levied fines against members who used profanity on the ball field.)

Cartwright's game, which became almost the private property of the Knickerbocker club, had other features that commended it to young men with only part of Sunday free for playing ball. His rule of "three-out, all-out" had the two sides competing neck and neck and so held the excitement high. In other two-sided ball games, the rule was often that an entire side of twenty or more would come to bat before the opposing side had a chance to hit. And even then the final batter might call for "the rounder" — and if he hit that ball far enough to tag all five bases before being hit, the whole side could come up *again*.

In Cartwright's game, the duration of the contest was limited by a rule that gave victory to the first side that scored twenty-one *aces* (runs) in even innings (so each side had an equal number of innings at bat). Innings were long enough, heaven knows, since no balls or strikes were called and the ball contained so much India rubber that home runs were commonplace. Twenty-one aces were sometimes scored in just three or four innings. Whereas a town-ball game might last from right after breakfast to long past time for supper, Cartwright's game was decided in plenty of time for the losers to treat the winners to a cold drink at a tavern nearby.

The improvements in the game that finally turned it into baseball — calling strikes and *wides* (balls), limiting the game to nine innings and nine players on each side (for a time there was a "shortstop" between first base and second base as well as between second and third), deadening the ball, lengthening the pitching distance, changing from a *square pitch* (underhand toss) to an overhand throw — all these were developed when the game was taken over by a rougher sort of young man, who sought more speed, more excitement, fiercer competition, and more deception. Most of the old Knickerbockers deplored this corruption of their private pastime. But Cartwright, an adventurous man all his life, continued to spread the gospel of baseball all over the land. He put in four years as a member of the Knickerbocker nine and often served as the club's umpire in match games. (Each club in those days had its own umpire to watch the play from a stool off to one side of home base and to call fouls and rule violations. When the umpires disagreed, the decision was referred to a neutral *referee* who made the final call.)

In 1849, when the nation was aroused by news of gold strikes in California, Cartwright and eleven companions, under the leadership of a man named D'Arcy, who was president of the Camden & Amboy Railroad, set out for the goldfields. They traveled by train to Pittsburgh, where they purchased a covered wagon and enough supplies to take them across the western plains. Alex, who was twenty-nine years old then and at the height of his vigor — a splendidly muscled man with a luxuriant black beard — took care to include among the supplies several bats and baseballs. They shipped wagon and supplies to Saint Louis, where Cartwright and company arrived forty-two days later. They had moseyed west in leisurely fashion, stopping often to demonstrate the New York game to young people throughout Pennsylvania, Ohio, Indiana, and Illinois.

In Independence, Missouri, five days after leaving Saint Louis, the Cartwright caravan chose a new leader, a veteran frontiersman and ex-soldier named Russell. He led them on, by foot and horseback, to Boundary, a frontier village in Indian territory where the Wild West really began. Here, while waiting for a wagon train to assemble, Cartwright and his friends taught baseball to the Indians and howled with glee as the beginners made awkward efforts to throw a baseball (bent-elbow fashion), swing a long skinny bat, or catch a flying ball with extended fingers. By the time he and his companions left Boundary, Alex Cartwright had grown into a perfect model of a modern forty-niner, with unkempt beard, trail-worn boots, dusty britches, deep-set dark eyes, and sun-tanned countenance. Tall, powerful, and ruddy with health, he won the respect of Indian and white man alike as he stalked among them like a king, towering over the entire company.

When they left Boundary, Cartwright chose to walk. He covered twenty-eight miles on foot in the first day and from that day forth, all the way to California, he walked about twenty miles a day. Alex could be seen marching along with long loping strides, still taking time during stopovers to get out on the prairie with the boys to show the frontier folk how to hit the baseball a mile.

In California, Alex met his brother, who had come by ship all the way around Cape Horn. They took counsel together and decided the goldfields were already overcrowded and that a better place for young men to seek their fortune might be the Sandwich Isles (later called Hawaii). So there they sailed, aboard a Peruvian ship, after only five days in California. And there Alexander Cartwright spent all the rest of his life teaching baseball in his leisure hours, not only to the sons of white planters but to the native children as well. Thanks to Cartwright's efforts, there was more baseball per square mile played in Hawaii for many years than there was on the mainland. Long before the Knickerbocker game grew into the National Game at home, it was the most popular pastime in Honolulu — planted and nurtured there by Alexander Cartwright, the man who drew the first diamond in the dirt and who worked as umpire in the first match game, played in Hoboken, New Jersey, in 1846.

The lords of professional baseball, however, did not get around to honoring the true father of their game until 1939 — at the same time that they celebrated the imaginary deeds of Abner Doubleday, who probably never played real baseball in his life, was never known to mention the game, and was never recorded as having even watched baseball being played. They put Cartwright in their new Hall of Fame, and left Doubleday out. In the same year, the Hawaiian government declared a Cartwright Day and a delegation of uniformed players from the Kauai League gathered at Cartwright's grave in Nuuanu to celebrate the fact that he had brought the New York game to Hawaii and had spread it throughout the islands — long before the kids in Cooperstown, New York, had even learned the rules.

WILLIAM HENRY (HARRY) WRIGHT

Father of Professional Baseball

There is still another ballplayer from the early days who was long known as "father of the game." He truly earned the title, for he was certainly father of professional baseball. He was Harry Wright, one of three brothers — Sam, Harry, and George. Sam and Harry were born in England and George in Harlem, New York. All played cricket professionally; Harry and George spent most of their lifetimes in professional baseball.

Harry, invited in 1868 to come to Cincinnati as cricket professional, there organized the first openly professional baseball club, the Cincinnati Red Stockings. The club was named after the bright red stockings made for it by a young lady named Margaret Truman. Actually, the Red Stockings, when first organized, were an "amateur" nine, in the style of the 1850s and 1860s: fake jobs were "arranged" for the players that permitted them to give full time to baseball. But Harry, who may have been influenced by Henry Chadwick's campaign against the hypocrisy of pretending that ballplayers were playing for love of

NATIONAL BASEBALL HALL OF FAME

Harry Wright

the game rather than for money, decided in 1869 to announce to the wondering world that *his* players were drawing salaries. Of course, hardly anyone ever believed that star amateur ballplayers were not being paid under the table. Al Reach, the famous Philadelphia slugger, openly bragged that he would join whatever team offered "the top dollar." But morality in those days was sometimes largely a matter of appearances, and most of the proper folk who came to baseball games required only that the players pretend that they had an honest way of making a living and were playing the game entirely for fun.

The game of baseball in 1869 was already growing into a true national pastime, with baseball clubs — some truly amateur, some make-believe amateur — in every corner of the nation. Still, Harry and his Red Stockings, in a tour of the East in 1869, made people everywhere wake up to the fact that baseball, unlike the roughhouse games boys of that day usually wasted their time on, could be fast, exciting, tightly played, and thrilling — even to sit and watch.

A visit by the Red Stockings invariably left behind a city full of boys who would try to imitate the tricks these great men had performed: catching the ball with the hands cupped and letting them "give," so the ball would not bounce out; swinging the long bat with the vigor of an ax, instead of pushing it like a broom; spinning the ball up to the batter (usually called the *striker*) with extra speed imparted by cocking the wrist. Little boys began to pester their mothers to let them buy baseball belts with shiny metal emblems on the buckles, or baseball hats with visors such as the great Red Stockings wore.

The Red Stockings gradually earned a special following throughout Cincinnati, which immediately became the capital of the baseball world. The local kranks (fans) chose to overlook the fact that the club was not made up of local lads, but rather of men who had all (except for one) been imported from all over the East. At least, the club's thousands of followers told themselves, the club had been organized by a Cincinnatian — Aaron B. Champion, who had vowed to develop a team that would be worthy of his name. And at least a native Cincinnatian, Charlie Gould, played first base.

The real star of the club was Harry Wright's kid brother, George, who played shortstop and drew the highest salary on the club ($1400 a season). George had played as a baseball "amateur" in New York and Washington. (His phony business address in Washington turned out to be a vacant lot — and not even a baseball lot.)

Harry himself was no great player, even though he once hit seven home runs in one game. In his day, almost every batter would make at least one home run and some would make three or four every game. The scores often exceeded a hundred runs in nine innings, because the ball was made mostly of rubber and would bounce high over a fielder's head when it struck the ground.

After a few victorious visits to outlying towns the Red Stockings became the darlings of all Cincinnati. When the train chugged in bringing the returning heroes, there was always a cheering crowd at the station to wave banners, toss flowers, fire off guns, and — with the accompaniment of a brass band hired for the occasion — join the ballplayers in singing the "team song":

Hurrah! Hurrah!
For our noble game, hurrah!
Red Stockings all, we'll toss the ball
And sing our loud hurrah!

The team was then escorted to beribboned carriages that transported all the players to a hotel, where a banquet had been planned in their honor. Speeches and songs and toasts took up most of the night; there were presents for every member of the club, and a trophy for the team. One party ended with the presentation of a giant baseball bat as long as the banquet table.

The Red Stockings even invaded New York City — to challenge the famous Mutual club, directed and financed by Boss Tweed. The game was played in Brooklyn, where most ball games were played in that era, because the location offered the extra room needed to accommodate the crowds. The Red Stockings won this game by the astounding score of 4 to 2 — only six runs scored in a game that ordinarily would see each side with thirty or forty scores recorded! Surely, the sportswriters allowed, there would never be another game like this, nor ever again two teams so wonderfully matched.

The Red Stockings became the acknowledged champions of the nation, but eventually ran into a team that outscored them — the great Atlantic club of Brooklyn. Actually, the outcome of the game was strongly influenced by an excited Brooklyn fan who at one point jumped upon the back of Cincinnati outfielder Cal McVey just as he was about to put away a high fly for an out. Just the same, the score stood and the Red Stockings were champions no longer.

"Defeated," Aaron Champion telegraphed his associates back in Cincinnati, "but not disgraced."

The burghers of Cincinnati (which was known to sportswriters and other irreverent people as Porkopolis) did not completely agree with Champion. Having savored the joy of being number one in the baseball world, they took no pleasure at all in a game in which they were rated number two or lower. Before very long the Red Stockings were drawing hardly enough spectators to pay the shortstop's salary, and it began to look as if it had been a mistake to admit that the team was simply a collection of hired hands, rather than a select group of native loyalists who were bound to lay down their lives — or at least their teeth and fingers — in defense of the city's honor.

When they first began to play ball together the Red Stockings had defeated the previous local heroes, the Buckeye club, so badly that the Buckeyes had simply dissolved as a team. Now the same fate loomed for the Red Stockings, since hardly anyone was willing to give them make-believe jobs that would allow them to be "amateurs" again. But Harry Wright was determined to hold his team of players together, even if they had to find other fields to play in. So he took off for

Boston, where baseball had long held the status of a local religion, and found sponsors there who would provide a park to play in and jobs of some sort for the players.

The players, however, had not all been able to wait for Harry to find them a new city, and most of them had gone back East to hook up with other amateur clubs. Only Charlie Gould, whose home was in Cincinnati, and George Wright, Harry's kid brother, were still available. Harry took them to Boston with him. He also gathered up and took along the red stockings Miss Truman had made for the club, so the new nine became the Boston Red Stockings.

Now that baseball players everywhere were imitating the way Harry's club dressed — including short pants (the early nines had worn long trousers, high shoes, and straw hats) — a number of teams named themselves after the color of their stockings. There were White Stockings in Chicago, and there soon appeared Browns in Saint Louis and Blues in Hartford, Connecticut. These names all faded out as the clubs disbanded or as sportswriters found new nicknames for them. The Boston Red Stockings became first the Reds, and then the Beaneaters; the Chicago White Stockings became the Colts, then the Orphans, and finally the Cubs. The Saint Louis Browns went out of business, as did the Hartford Blues, who played most of their games in Brooklyn. Many years later, new clubs in a new league, trying to awaken old loyalties, took some of the names back and altered them a little, to Red Sox in Boston and White Sox in Chicago. And for a time the Browns were revived in Saint Louis. Actually, the Chicago club had agreed, after a threat of a law suit, not even to use the name "Chicago," so they adopted a short version of the famous old name — White *Sox* instead of *Stockings* — to make sure people knew where they came from.

Harry Wright ran the Boston club for eleven years. Although he yielded at first to the sponsors' insistence that it would be fatal to the club's chances to admit to being professionals, Harry, after one season, grew sick of the hypocrisy and told everyone out loud that he was paying his players. And when the census taker came around, Harry proudly listed his occupation as "Base Ball Player."

Harry soon took himself out of the club's lineup and confined himself to managing. A patient, invariably gentle man, with a quiet and sympathetic manner, Harry could keep even the most intractable young athlete in harness. Like all good managers, he advised against chafing players in public if they needed correction. His style was always to call them aside and gently correct them in private. And in his years in the National Association of Professional Baseball Players, and later in the National League, Harry had to deal with many of the toughest characters in the game. The spectators, too, in the 1870s, began to comport themselves in rowdy fashion, and women were strongly advised to stay away from baseball parks, where rival fans (a new name derived from *fancy,* which had been used for followers of cockfighting and prizefighting) often hurled rocks and whiskey bottles at each other, or even at the players, when sectional rivalry ran high.

Harry, however, remained his gentle self — respected by everyone, always just and fair, and loved by veteran ballplayers and youngsters alike. When the Boston club, after some of its best players deserted to Chicago, began to lose games and followers, Harry moved to Providence, Rhode Island, where he managed the local club for two years, and finally to Philadelphia, where he stayed for ten. He won no more league pennants, but he always brought his team home close to the top, and he remained a father figure to the whole league.

In his playing days Harry had worn a set of luxuriant whiskers that would have been the envy of even an Oakland outfielder today — long hair, sideburns, and heavy mustache. In his later years, he grew a little beard to go with them, so that he looked, when his whiskers began to grow gray, more like the game's grandfather.

Harry was finally eased out of the game by the owners of the Philadelphia club, who awarded him a "lifetime pass" instead of a pension. But he did not disappear from the game. In Boston, in competition with his younger brother George, who had founded the sporting-goods firm of Wright & Ditson, Harry began a similar business with a partner named Mahn. And he became known everywhere as an expert on organizing, operating, and managing a ball club. After his retirement, and long after the firm of Wright & Mahn had vanished, men all over the country wrote asking Harry for help or advice in getting ball clubs started, and fans of his from everywhere wrote letters to the league insisting that Harry be kept in the game. Finally, the club owners gave in and created for Harry a job as "supervisor of umpires" at a small salary. In that capacity, Harry continued to send out his patient advice on whether to let wives come to baseball games for free, on where to get tickets printed, and on what exercises and diet were best for improving endurance, strengthening the throwing arm, or sharpening the batting eye.

Harry was only sixty when he died, but in a sense he had already had an opportunity to enjoy his own funeral. Some years earlier, when his eyesight had begun to fail, it had been rumored throughout baseball that Harry Wright was dying, and he received gifts, letters, and telegrams from nearly every state in the Union, mostly from old ballplayers — former teammates and opponents alike — who had played with Harry in his best days. The ballplayers never lost their respect for old Harry or their devotion to him, even though he had seemingly betrayed their cause by refusing to join the Players' Brotherhood strike in 1890. Harry had refused simply because the Players' League, which the strikers had organized, played games on Sunday — and that was against Harry's principles. The players knew that and respected Harry for it.

ALBERT GOODWILL (A. G.) SPALDING

Father of the National League

Al Spalding, the true organizer of the National League of Professional Baseball Clubs (today's National League), supposedly became a baseball player because he once retrieved a hard-hit baseball at a game between amateur clubs and impressed everyone with the speed and accuracy with which he threw the ball back. The incident, it is said, occurred during the Civil War, in a day when boys who could throw a baseball with accuracy were not found in every backyard. For whatever reason, Al Spalding, a lanky boy with prominent ears, was invited, before he was even a teenager, to become a member of the local boys' baseball nine. (In those days, a nine was truly a nine — no substitutes were allowed, and the relief, or *change,* pitcher, if there was one, usually played in right field until he was needed.)

The club Al joined was the Pioneers of Rockford, Illinois, fifteen miles from his home. He had been visiting an aunt in Rockford when he made his unscheduled debut, moving from a spectator's seat to a steady place in the lineup of the Pioneers, who were said to be the best boys' baseball team west of the Hudson River. They were certainly the best in the Chicago area, and soon had trouble finding any teenage club they could not beat by resounding scores. After two years of whipping all the kids' nines in sight, the Pioneers challenged the Rockford Mercantiles, a group of grown-up young men who worked as clerks in the local shops.

Pressured by the ridicule of their neighbors, the Mercantiles, who had at first laughed off the challenge, finally agreed to meet the little fellows. They soon wished they hadn't, for young pitcher Al Spalding tied their strikers in knots. In nine innings, the shamed clerks could collect only two runs off fourteen-year-old Spalding, while Al's team scored twenty-six. (And this was in a day, remember, when twenty-six runs was a moderate score.)

Among the delighted spectators that day were many of the members of the really big club in Rockford, the Forest Cities — all amateurs who accepted undercover payment for playing ball. They immediately invited Al Spalding to join their team. Al hesitated. He had to go to school in the afternoon! And his aunt was not going to allow him to play hooky just to waste his time on a baseball diamond. The leaders of the Forest City club, however, paid a visit to the principal of Al's school, and the school official readily agreed to allow Al to leave school on game days at two o'clock. The principal was himself a baseball krank, it seems, and he too planned to hop down to the field at that hour.

With Al in the *pitcher's point* — there was no mound in those days, just a sort of marked-off area — the Forest Cities became invincible. When school was over, they arranged to keep Al by fixing it with a local grocer to give Al a job at four dollars a week. The Forest Cities, after beating all the clubs within a reasonable carriage ride, even dared to challenge the mightiest team in the state — the great Excelsior club of Chicago. (In that day, every major city would field many baseball clubs — even as many as fifty — representing almost every profession in town, from milk peddlers to policemen.) The Forest Cities could not quite overcome the Excelsiors, but they provided competition stiff enough to earn high ranking in the area.

So when the famous National club of Washington, D.C., came to the Chicago area on the first cross-country tour by any baseball team, a challenge was issued to the Forest Cities, in hopes that the small-towners might provide the Nationals a good workout before their major contest with the Excelsiors.

There was no stronger team in the nation then than the Nationals, who had been organized by Colonel Frank Jones of the War Department. Most of the great, big-name players of the East had been appointed to government jobs so they could play ball for Colonel Jones. Leading the club was George Wright, hitter and fielder extraordinary, destined to become the most famous shortstop in the Union. The Nationals, on this tour, had already beaten the Cincinnati team (not yet called the Red Stockings), the Louisville team, the Western club of Indianapolis, and both the Empires and the Unions of Saint Louis.

The game with the Forest Cities was played July 25, 1867, at Dexter Park in Chicago, before an enormous crowd, most of whom had gathered just to watch the wonders the Nationals might work. What they saw was a miracle performed by sixteen-year-old Al Spalding, who, despite some nervousness at the start, stifled the Nationals, holding them to a mere twenty-three runs, while the Forest Cities scored twenty-nine. News of this amazing score was sent out by wire to the whole nation, while local kranks succumbed to delirium. It seemed obvious to all now that the really *great* local club, the Excelsiors, would make dogmeat of these easterners.

The huge crowd at the Forest City game had barely fit into the park, so the Excelsiors, to hold down attendance at the real showdown, set a fee of fifty cents to come see their club stage the massacre. (It was considered bad form to charge admission to baseball games at that time. The Nationals scorned any payment beyond a lavish banquet after the game — the fifty-cent charge was imposed just to keep the crowd down.) But the Nationals spoiled the afternoon by walloping the Excelsiors 49 to 4. It could not be! several sportswriters proclaimed; the Nationals had obviously dumped the game with the Forest Cities to improve the betting odds! (Even umpires openly bet on ball games in the 1860s.)

When this charge was printed in the Chicago *Tribune,* Colonel Jones, with his black whiskers bristling, marched into the *Tribune* office and forced a retraction. The Nationals had played their *hearts* out to beat Spalding and his Forest City teammates. Why, Colonel Jones himself, near the end of the game, had stomped out onto the field as George Wright, the Nationals' mightiest hitter, came up to bat, and had personally urged him: "Use a lighter bat, George! We're getting beat! The whole trip will be ruined!" But a lighter bat availed poor George nothing against the wiles of Al Spalding.

So, it was obvious this Spalding boy was one of the greatest pitchers in the country. The Excelsiors promptly approached Al to offer a new job, with a wholesale grocer in Chicago, at *forty* dollars a week instead of four. Al did not even have to ask his aunt's permission to make that deal. He promptly quit school and went to Chicago.

But alas, the wholesale grocer who was so ready to hire young men at ten times the going wage and then let them off work to play baseball went bankrupt after Spalding had pitched only one game for his new club. By the time the next baseball season opened, Al Spalding was back in Rockford, looking for work. His search was promptly rewarded by the Forest Cities, who found *two* jobs for him — neither one of which would interfere with his pitching. With Al back on the point, the Forest Cities again grew mighty in battle and even managed to sink the great Atlantics of Brooklyn and the Philadelphia Athletics (the "old" Athletics, not the team that was revived much later, after the game had changed almost beyond recognition).

Rockford tradesmen now began to brag of "their" Forest Cities to everyone they met, and they finally collected a fat pot to finance a national tour for the team. Spalding by now was as famous as any of the great eastern stars and could count on drawing out crowds in almost any town. He even led his club into Washington, D.C., and beat the Nationals all over again, then traveled to Cincinnati and beat the fading Red Stockings. His meeting there with Harry Wright altered the course of Al's life for good. Harry, soon after their meeting, set out to move his club to Boston, and he invited Al Spalding to come take the job of pitcher. From the time his club had faced the Red Stockings, the only openly professional club in the country, Al Spalding had been taken with the idea of making a real profession out of ball playing. This pretending to be a bookkeeper or a grocery clerk was more than his nature could bear. So he hastened to sign with the Boston Red Stockings, accepting a $500 advance against a $1500 salary. He also brought along with him, from the Forest Cities, Ross Barnes, famed as a batter chiefly because of his skill at delivering "fair-foul" hits—bunts that under the rules were fair because they landed fair, even though they might roll off deep among the spectators before they could be fielded.

Spalding was annoyed, as Harry Wright himself was, at the devices that had to be cooked up to slip salaries to players who were still pretending to be amateurs, and he joined Harry in defying Boston traditions by proclaiming himself a professional baseball player. Almost at once, the other great clubs began to cast off their disguises, and before long they all had joined to form the National Association of Professional Baseball Players.

In Boston, Spalding earned his greatest fame. He became feared among ballplayers and renowned among fans for his dazzling change of pace — a tantalizing slow pitch delivered with exactly the same motion as the fastball. He was Boston's only pitcher and he worked every day. In his first season he won 21 games out of 33. The next year he won 36 out of 48. In his fourth season he won 41 out of 60, then 52 out of 71 the following year. In 1875, Al took to playing first base part of the time, but still won 55 games out of 61 pitched.

No longer the skinny, lop-eared boy who could put his elders to shame, Al Spalding was now the very picture of an athletic hero, and he seemed quite aware of the figure he cut. A muscular man, with meat on his frame and a small mustache to proclaim his masculinity, Spalding used to pose so often in the pitcher's box — Greek-statue style, with the ball held in both hands just under his chin and his feet placed like a dancer's — that spectators and rival players used to laugh out loud at him. The laughter stopped when Al began to pitch, for rare indeed was the batter who could make a solid safe hit off him.

The game of baseball itself, however, was going to pot. Ever since the first organized match game, staged by the Knickerbockers, gambling had been a fixture of the contest — openly engaged in by players and spectators and even umpires. By the time the professional players had organized themselves into a league, the fixing of games had become so brazen that newspapers specifically accused one team or another of selling out to the gamblers. And some ballplayers took to publicly flaunting the extra greenbacks they had earned by letting a few enemy runs score.

Al Spalding — whose ambition was soaring and who had long

THE BETTMANN ARCHIVE

A young Al Spalding in the uniform of the Boston team

dreamed of a tightly organized league in which play would be honest and salaries high (and where he, like teammate George Wright, might find a market for baseball equipment) — used to spend most of his idle hours working out schemes for reforming the organized game. One of his sweetest dreams pictured a voyage to England by American baseball figures, with Al Spalding leading, to demonstrate baseball to the sporting folk in the mother country. He may even have hoped he could establish the game there and develop international competition. A number of sportswriters — including the great Henry Chadwick, who had long held that baseball was a British game in spirit and in origin —

helped sell several wealthy sportsmen on the idea that England was clamoring to see what the Americans had made out of rounders and that Spalding was just the gentleman to journey overseas and arrange for several matches. Spalding sailed to England, but found there almost no desire to underwrite such a spectacle — a contest between two groups of Americans in a game that, for all the British knew, might have been invented by the Indians, to be played with tomahawks. But Al Spalding, with his long experience in dealing with negative calls by umpires, managed to persuade the leaders of the Marylebone Cricket Club that what the Americans wanted most to do was meet the British in *cricket.* (There were, indeed, a number of skilled cricket players on the Boston and Philadelphia baseball clubs.)

So the tour was arranged. The Americans, who were granted some slight advantages to compensate for their inexperience, managed to beat the British in cricket. They also bewildered the English sporting fancy with their exhibition of baseball, bored the Prince of Wales almost into a stupor (he could not even begin to follow the unfamiliar game), and impressed the London press with their appearance and manners: "almost gentlemanly," with no tobacco chewing, nor any *consarn it*s or *Jumping Jehoshaphat*s. They were banqueted everywhere and endlessly cheered, and they sailed home to a triumphal welcome.

This success fed Spalding's ambition so much that he could no longer be content as a mere pitcher of baseballs. He found a wealthy baseball krank from Chicago named William Hulbert and talked him into backing Spalding's scheme for getting professional baseball back on its feet. Hulbert, a longtime supporter of the Chicago White Stockings, urged Spalding to come back to Chicago, at a *decent* salary. (There had been no extra money in Spalding's pocket despite the successes of the Boston Reds.) Spalding agreed and brought back three of his Boston teammates with him, including Ross Barnes.

This was the very first wholesale defection from any baseball club by its stars. It was greeted by sportswriters and especially by Boston fans as if it were a form of treachery as deep-dyed as military desertion in the face of the enemy. There had been "shooting-stars" in baseball before, and they were scolded in the press for changing their loyalties in exchange for so vulgar a lure as mere cash in the pocket. But never had any club seen the heart of its lineup succumb to the temptation of money all in one swoop.

But no amount of bad press or dirty names cast at them by small boys in Boston streets could deter Spalding and Hulbert; they were determined to take hold of the game of baseball and remake it even despite protests from other clubs, and they vowed they would have their way, even if the entire players' association tried to stand against them. As other club owners saw their players straining at the leash, they quickly agreed to cooperate with the two reformers. Spalding and Hulbert pulled out of a desk drawer a blueprint for a new organization — not of baseball players, but of baseball *clubs,* with the final authority in the hands of management. They intended to eradicate open gambling and liquor selling, to expel clubs that failed to stick to schedules, and to turn the organized game back into a pastime that decent folk would not be ashamed to bring their families to watch.

Thus, in 1876, was the National League founded. Some clubs dropped out and new clubs were admitted. There were times when the whole league looked as if it might founder. William Hulbert devoutly hoped the league might last a mere five years, but it has survived for more than a hundred. Spalding became team manager in Chicago and pitched only one more season, winning 47 games out of 66. He put in two seasons as part-time infielder, then retired to the executive offices of the club. He was not yet thirty, but he found himself adding flab to his middle and losing a little agility in his arms and legs, so he backed out before he could disgrace himself.

Having resolved to make baseball his entire livelihood, Spalding was constantly on the lookout for new sources of income from the game. Before leaving Boston he had made a secret deal with Harry Wright's business partner (the fellow named Mahn) to act as Mahn's agent in Chicago. But once well-established there, Spalding set up a new business of his own, with his nineteen-year-old brother, Walter, ostensibly in charge. A. G. Spalding and brother immediately began a thriving trade in sporting goods. Before long, Al took in his brother-in-law as well and incorporated the business as A. G. Spalding & Brothers.

As one of the founders and one of the most influential club managers in the new league, Al Spalding had little difficulty in selling the league his new promotional idea: he offered to pay the league a dollar for each dozen Spalding baseballs used in league play, if they would name the Spalding ball the "official" ball of the league. After years of paying high prices for baseballs, which were so valuable that games would be often delayed for an hour while everyone looked for a lost ball, the club owners in the new National League could hardly believe their good fortune. Not just *free* baseballs, but a bonus of a dollar a dozen! They promptly designated the Spalding ball the official baseball of the National League. For a hundred years, it remained so.

Spalding also worked out the territorial scheme that prevented clubs from competing for the same group of fans in towns too close together. This scheme encouraged the growth of the minor leagues and thus established an excellent training ground for skilled players who could later be promoted into the National League. Spalding also led the battle against the Players' Brotherhood, which, in 1890, called the first

NATIONAL BASEBALL HALL OF FAME

A. G. Spalding, the elder statesman of baseball

players' strike. Using much the same sort of tricky argument, fast talk and deception that had marked his career as a pitcher, bully of umpires, and salesman for the game, Spalding managed to con the organized players into surrender when actually his own forces were on the verge of collapse.

When he eventually became the elder statesman of the game as publisher of the official *National League Guide* (he paid the league a premium to let him use that designation, too), it was hard to picture A. G. Spalding as a former athlete. He was portly, impressively dressed, and had, some people said, "the manner of a bishop." And there is no question he was the dominant figure in baseball. Through boldness and high-handedness (he single-handedly removed league papers from the league office and secreted them in his own), he managed to defeat a group of club owners who favored "syndicate" baseball, which would have allowed them to own several clubs and to shift players around to wherever the most money could be made. Spalding also promoted the Abner Doubleday legend and pretended that he really believed it, although privately he thought it was nonsense.

And once, when he found himself barred from a sold-out ball park in New York (the police were not letting in any of the thousands who milled outside the gate), Spalding got in by tailgating an ambulance and slipping through the police line before the gate could be shut in front of him. All his life, he had been quick at finding ways to bring Al Spalding in first.

MICHAEL J. (KING) KELLY

The Ten-Thousand-Dollar Beauty

In the last century, it was the style to name a leader in any activity a king. There were kings of the racetrack and kings of second basemen. But there was not a baseball krank in all America in the 1880s who would not have known, when anyone spoke of the King of the Diamond, that he meant Mike Kelly of Chicago — infielder, outfielder, catcher, pitcher, mighty batsman, and demon base runner — for Mike never failed to dominate the whole scene when he took the field wearing his baseball uniform. He was really not a big man (only five-foot-ten) but fans always seemed to remember him as the tallest and widest and strongest man on the field.

Mike always loudly enjoyed the game, cooking up new stratagems to drive umpires and rule makers crazy, taunting the opposition, cracking jokes with the fans, and celebrating all his small successes and failures with flamboyant gestures. And above all, he was the greatest slider alive. He is the Kelly whose name still lives in the catch phrase

NATIONAL BASEBALL HALL OF FAME

Mike Kelly

"Slide, Kelly, slide!" — for that is what the fans used to shout in unison once Mike Kelly got on base.

Mike seldom disappointed them; he loved to slide and always seemed to have some new way of performing the stunt. His basic slide was supposedly his own invention. Known as the *spread slide* or the *Chicago slide* in Mike's day, it was really a hook slide, in which the body heads away from the base and one foot is left trailing to hook the base in passage. Infielders in Mike's era, who saw mostly headfirst sliding if they saw any at all, were accustomed to bending over and making the tag on the runner's ribs. But what if the runner's ribs were way off to the side somewhere, out of reach? Time and time again second basemen who waited to tag Mike Kelly were left standing with mouth open and the ball clutched uselessly in one hand.

If a baseman prepared for Mike's slide by bending over and holding the ball near the base in order to tag Mike on the foot, Mike was very likely to kick the ball right out of the baseman's hand. Or he might decide to go right on past the base and reach back to tag it with his fingers.

Now and then, if a base hit to right field was holding the lone umpire's attention, Mike might shorten his trip around the bases after rounding second by leaving third base out altogether and cutting for the plate along a route just to the third-base side of the pitcher's mound. By the time the distracted umpire awoke to the fact that there might be funny business afoot behind him, Mike would be triumphantly stamping one foot on the plate for the score and there would be no telling whether he had tagged third base or not — except that all the opposition players would be yelling blue murder.

Tricks like this always used to delight or enrage the fans, depending on whether they were on Mike's side or against him. But often he would win over the enemy, too — they could not help laughing at Mike's tricks. For instance, because the rule makers had forgotten to put in a rule to prevent base runners from leaving the base paths on their way from base to base, Mike used to take pleasure in taking the scenic route home when the ball had been hit out of sight. A home run lost in deep grass or even in a creek in those days was more common than one hit over the fence. One day, when a ball he had hit could not be found immediately, Mike solemnly trotted out into the outfield and ran in a semicircle around each fielder on his way from base to base. *Everybody* laughed at that, even the enemy players.

Mike also realized that there was no rule in his day requiring that base runners proceed around the bases in order without passing one another, so sometimes when there was a runner behind him he stopped dead in his tracks within a stride of home plate and let the runner following him slide home first through the arch formed by his outspread legs.

When he was playing defense, Mike had other tricks. The invention of the catcher's mask in the 1870s provided Mike with just another weapon. He used to drop his mask on home plate when a runner was coming in and thus force a detour that would give Mike time to get the throw and make the tag. One day, Mike was playing outfield in a game that had lasted until twilight. His team was ahead, about to wrap up the victory, when with two out in the ninth a batter sent a long line drive out in Mike's direction. Mike leaped several feet into the dusk to snag the ball and then came trotting silently in toward the bench. The umpire, peering out into the murky outfield, signaled the out, and the teams began to gather up their bats. Mike's boss met him at the bench and asked for the ball — baseballs being too valuable then to allow any to be wasted. "The ball?" Mike growled. "It went a mile over me head!"

But Mike was far more than a trickster. He could hit the ball often and hard, throw it powerfully, and dog it down like a starving hound. There was really nothing required of a baseball player that Mike could not do. He had started playing baseball as a small boy and never wanted to do anything else for a living. He relished his fame, lavishly tossed his salary around, and enjoyed good company, good food, and good drink. Cap Anson, his manager in Chicago, used to keep Mike away from the bar and the banquet table during the season so that Mike was just bone and muscle all summer long. But in the off-season Mike would give himself to jollity and sometimes had many pounds to sweat off in the spring.

Born in Lansingburgh (Troy), New York — the town made famous in baseball circles by the Troy Haymakers — Mike moved to Washington before he was ten, when his father, a soldier, was transferred there right after the Civil War. While most kids in Washington were still playing burn ball, Mike very early joined a club of preteens who called themselves the Keystones and played the New York version of the game. When his father had to retire from the army, the family moved to Paterson, New Jersey, where young Mike organized another baseball team, which he named the Keystones. They were a haphazard collection of teenagers, with only a few pieces of baseball equipment among them. But one of them did own a baseball cap — a fifteen-center — and Mike dearly desired to wear it. The cap was an exact replica of the one worn by Mike's personal hero, Big Joe Start, the "Old Reliable" first baseman of the New York Mutuals. So Mike, finding he was the fastest runner, hardest hitter, and best catcher on the club, insisted that he be given the cap in exchange for playing with the nine in match games.

The Keystones grew up together and eventually included some of the best ballplayers in the area. Their pitcher was Edward Nolan, a young railroad fireman who later became famous throughout the land as The Only Nolan, the man who pitched thirty shutouts in one season for Indianapolis and posted an earned run average of 0.50 — just half a run per nine-inning game. For the first three years that the Keystones played together, Nolan did all the pitching and Kelly all the catching.

The Keystones traveled all over New Jersey, meeting "independent" nines (amateur or semipro) and beating most of them. They played, like most teams of their type, on a cooperative basis, equally splitting the proceeds gained from passing the hat at games. Sometimes there would be only three dollars to divide among the players. This was hardly enough to keep young Mike Kelly's soul attached to his body — he had to find a regular job of some sort. His father had died when Mike was sixteen and when his mother died soon after, Mike had to make his own living. He tried working in the local silk mill, like so many other young men in his neighborhood. But that was too confining for him, and the three-dollar-a-week wage was hardly tempting. Mike soon found a job bringing New York newspapers down to Paterson on the early morning train. This meant getting up at four in the morning — but it also meant he had the whole afternoon to play ball.

After Nolan graduated to professional baseball, Mike Kelly teamed up with Jim McCormick, another mighty pitcher, who was destined to become manager of the Cleveland Spiders of the National League. (Jim was no spider, though — he weighed 225 pounds.) Kelly and McCormick soon became famous in eastern cities as the "Keystone Battery" and they earned attention from owners of professional clubs. Mike, after making a halfhearted effort one winter to learn the silk-weaver's trade, signed up with the pro team at Port Jervis, New York, earning money enough to keep meat on his table. He very soon had an offer from a big-league team — the Cincinnati Buckeyes of the National League — and he joined them soon after the start of the 1878 season.

Overcome by nervousness or homesickness or both, Kelly had a hard time holding on with the Buckeyes, who were experiencing a bad spell themselves. In his first twenty-one times at bat, while the club was losing to Troy, Syracuse, Providence, and Boston, Mike reached first base just once — on an error. Cal McVey, the new Buckeye manager, sent word to Manchester, New Hampshire, calling for a replacement outfielder to come bolster the Cincinnati lineup. "I'll get rid of either Kelly or Dickerson," he told his associates. This information quickly reached Mike's ever-alert ears, and he feared he was finished in the big leagues. Lew Dickerson, known as "Buttercup," had been ill, but he had still done better at bat than Kelly had.

Desperate at the thought of spending his remaining days in a silk mill, Mike Kelly went to bat next day with his heart full of determination. He hit the ball safely every time he came to bat, collecting two doubles, a triple, and a home run. His job was secure. To celebrate the return of his batting eye, Kelly in the next game (in which the Buckeyes beat Chicago) drove in every run his club scored.

Mike Kelly had no more spells of nervousness in baseball, although he did, a number of times, appear on the field with a hangover not quite healed. In the fall of 1879, he traveled to California with a group of stars from Buffalo and Cincinnati, and while there he helped give a thorough beating to the most famous "traveling" club of the day, the independent Hop Bitters team (named after a patent medicine made in Rochester, New York). Cap Anson of Chicago saw Mike's performance that day and promptly set out to induce young Kelly to come join the White Stockings. They wasted a week arguing over a hundred-dollar difference in salary before Cap gave in and took the young man back to Chicago with him. There was no rule then to prevent one club from hiring players away from another team — except for five key players that each club was allowed to "reserve."

It was in Chicago that Kelly became the King — known by teammates and fans alike as "King Kell." Mike seemed to cut a dashing figure anywhere he appeared — on the street, in his gleaming new civilian suit and florid cravat with a sparkling stickpin; or on the diamond, where he made his presence known with his cheery voice, his sharp tongue, his loud bat, and his flying feet. Within two or three seasons he was the most famous baseball player in America, and he soon realized a childhood dream — appearing on stage to tell baseball stories. He related them with enthusiasm and savored the audience response: wild applause, screams for more, and the chant "Slide, Kelly, slide!" For a finale, Kelly specialized in reciting "Casey at the Bat" to the delighted howls of the audience, who believed that "Casey" was probably Kelly himself.

Kelly, even in plain clothes, was a striking man, with abundant black hair that was always gleaming and falling in a wave. He sported a heavy mustache, a suntanned complexion, eyes eternally a-twinkle, and a mouth always ready to smile. Kelly played seven years for Cap Anson, as infielder, outfielder, catcher, and occasional pitcher. He took part in a winner-take-all series in 1886 against the Saint Louis Browns, which Chicago lost when Curt Welch of Saint Louis slid home under a wild pitch by Bobby Carruthers. Catcher Kelly signaled the defeat when, after leaping in vain for the ball, he hurled his mask and glove high into the air.

Kelly always enjoyed playing in Saint Louis, especially when he played the outfield and had an opportunity to trade insults with the Irish Catholic fans from the Saint Louis Kerry Patch who filled the bleachers. Kelly would make a point of inviting them all to meet him at Orangeman's Hall, a Protestant spot where no decent Catholic Irishman would allow even his corpse to be seen. And he would playfully invite them on occasion to join him in a chorus of "The Battle of the Boyne Water," a song that celebrates the defeat of the Irish by their Protestant foe. Kelly himself was Irish, of course, so the fans knew it was all in fun and no blows were ever struck.

Of course, no man as handsome and as free-spending as Mike Kelly could walk the streets of Chicago or enter its taverns without getting more than his share of attention from the girls — attention that Kelly never shunned. And it was said that his interest in the ladies helped prompt Cap Anson finally, in 1886, to sell Kelly to the Boston Reds — for ten thousand dollars, an unheard of price at that time. There was a stage lady of that day who, because of the salary she commanded, was known as "The Ten-Thousand-Dollar Beauty." When the price paid for Kelly was announced, the sportswriters promptly nicknamed Kelly "The Ten-Thousand-Dollar Beauty," and he wore that borrowed tag for several seasons.

In Boston, Kelly's ability shone as brightly as ever and he cut as dashing a figure on Tremont Street as ever he had on State Street in Chicago. His Boston fans all chipped in one time to buy Kelly a pair of matched gray horses and a carriage to go with them, and he took pride in spinning about town in this rig, grinning and acknowledging the greetings of his admirers. On the diamond he wore a uniform that seemed whiter than any other on the field, with letters across his chest that must have been half an inch thick.

Kelly was in Boston when the Brotherhood (Players' League) strike of 1890 began and he never thought twice about walking out with his colleagues. But his influence with other players was so great that A. G. Spalding made a special trip to offer Kelly a fat "bonus" to quit the Brotherhood and come back to the National League. Spalding and Kelly met in a hotel room, where Spalding offered Kelly a National League contract with the salary figure blank — ready to be filled in with almost any figure Kelly desired. And he tantalized Kelly with a check for ten thousand dollars — the bonus for signing — made out to "Michael J. Kelly."

Kelly, a big spender, was no man to scorn a fat paycheck. Quite often his pay envelope was full of cancelled IOUs, for Mike was always drawing ahead on his salary, so he could always use an extra ten-spot or two. He had never in his life seen ten thousand dollars in a single bundle, right in his own hand.

"I'll have to go out for a walk," he mumbled.

Kelly was gone for nearly an hour. When he came back his face was grim.

"I won't take it," he growled. "I can't go back on the boys." And he never did.

There were others, however, who did go back on the boys, succumbing to temptations far less glittering. One by one the backers of the Players' League were lured away by Spalding's crew, sometimes with promises that were never kept. So the strike finally collapsed. Kelly, however, stayed loyal and never knew a moment's regret.

After the Players' League expired, King Kell continued to play in Boston for part of a season with the Boston National League club and with the Boston club in the American Association. Then he was persuaded to transfer to the Cincinnati club in the American Association, to become manager and catcher.

The club he played with in Cincinnati, across the Ohio River from the National League club, was an assortment of eccentrics that might have been recruited by Kelly himself, for they seemed to make up their own rules and devoted themselves more religiously to the postgame banquet than they ever did to a ball game. Sometimes a few of the players would fail to make the scene in time for a game, and the team would play with only seven players on the field. But the banquet afterward, set out on a long table with a white linen cloth, always drew a capacity crowd, and there was always food and drink enough to keep all the players occupied until the late moon had risen.

Kelly called this crowd of free souls "Kelly's Killers," although they never threatened bodily harm, even to a mouse. They played games against teams of citizens more sober than themselves, sometimes beating them but often losing — and usually by scores that ran into double figures. Their best player, besides Kelly, was the pitcher, "Cannonball"

Ed Crane — a powerful lad from Boston, who had played for the short-lived Union Association club in that city and for Jim Mutrie's Giants in New York, as well as for Brooklyn and Washington. Crane was strong enough, it was said, to throw a baseball through a bale of hay. He did indeed strike out more than 170 batters for Kelly's team, but he walked over 200. Cannonball Ed did his finest work at the banquet table — where he even kept up with King Kelly.

Kelly's Killers eventually expired for lack of patronage. It was hard for Cincinnati's National League fans to get transportation across the river to see a game and was even harder to get back. So Kelly returned to the Boston Beaneaters of the National League. But Kelly, with no Cap Anson to sweat him into shape, had been putting in too much playtime at the table and the bar. He occasionally showed up at the ball park unable to steer a straight course. One day, after circling in vain under an easy fly ball and missing it completely, he boasted: "Well, by God, I made it hit me glove!" He was unable, however, to make the ball hit his bat often enough to earn his keep. His batting average fell to .189.

The Boston management could not sell Mike, but they arranged with the New York Giants to accept Kelly "on loan." Mike played twenty games with the Giants, and in that time attracted more attention in the night spots along Broadway than he did on the diamond. He was gay and carefree as ever, confident of his ability to start hitting the ball in his wonted way almost any time he desired. But the fans who used to applaud and laugh at his antics began to boo him now, and the New York club returned him, without thanks, to Boston, where he was no longer welcome.

Kelly then accepted a job as player-manager with the minor-league club in Allentown, Pennsylvania, where he expected the grateful small-town fans to greet him uproariously, as they always had when he was in his prime.

But the King's reputation just would not stretch to cover his many errors and his feeble efforts at the plate. Having spent so much of his youthful vigor in joyous celebration of his popularity and success, Kelly had begun to fail physically now and had to console himself even more liberally with drink and good company. He finally fled from the jeers of the Allentown fans and set himself up in business in New York as a saloon keeper, in partnership with "Honest John" Kelly, a former National League umpire. This project lasted about as long as any business does when one of the partners is bent on consuming the profits right on the premises.

Mike next tried a tour in vaudeville. He had grown accustomed to hearing a roar of applause whenever he walked on stage, and he still expected a half-dozen thunderous curtain calls after he finished reciting "Casey at the Bat." But the once-popular verse was no longer a novelty to theatergoers (it had been going the rounds for more than five years and was being offered by far more accomplished performers than Kelly). Moreover, poor Mike's deteriorating appearance no longer thrilled young fans. His shows on the tour were thinly attended and won only a smattering of applause, but Mike stuck doggedly to the schedule. He had to — he was thirty-seven now and had no future in baseball as a player.

On his way by boat to a performing engagement in Boston, Mike came down with pneumonia. He was carried off the boat on a stretcher and not much later died under an oxygen tent at the Boston City Hospital.

Mike's legacy to baseball is considerable. Not only did he force changes in the rules to prevent his wandering from the base paths and dropping his mask on the plate, but he turned sliding into a science and made the maneuver popular throughout baseball. He also, it was said, introduced the practice of having the catcher signal the pitcher to indicate desired pitches, and demonstrated, to the dismay of a number of absentminded hitters, that it is possible to play a short right field against right-handed batters and throw them out at first base if they do not run hard enough on a line drive over the first baseman's head. (Mike, playing shallow right field, often used to get right in behind the baseline between first and second and field such blows like an infielder.) Above all, Mike Kelly also reminded ballplayers, both amateur and professional, that baseball is fun — whether you win or lose.

JOHN MONTGOMERY (MONTE) WARD

Gentleman John

One day, when James Mutrie was watching his New York Baseball Club perform in the field, he stood up and opened his arms as if he would enfold them all.

"My big fellows!" he cried out. "My Giants!"

And thus he gave the club the name it has worn ever since — even after moving to San Francisco, three thousand miles away.

Jim Mutrie's Giants, however, were not *all* outsize men like Roger Connor, the six-foot-three first baseman; Pete Gillespie, the six-foot-one left fielder; or six-foot Joseph "Move Up Joe" Gerhardt, the second baseman. In that day when a man five-foot-ten would call himself tall, the Giants had a five-foot-nine outfielder-shortstop named John Montgomery Ward. And though not the tallest, Monte Ward may have been the toughest Giant of them all.

Not that John Ward looked, dressed, or behaved in a rowdy manner. He was indeed the man most often pointed out when polite fans wanted to prove that baseball players could be gentlemen. A graduate of

NATIONAL BASEBALL HALL OF FAME

Monte Ward

Pennsylvania State College, he was learned in the law and could hold his own in conversation, be it at a Park Avenue tea party or at a meeting of bankers. He dressed in neat and expensive clothes when off the diamond, and lived far from the ball park, in the fashionable Metropolitan Hotel, with his wife, the actress Helen Daubray. He was "a gentleman from sole to crown" — straight, handsome, well spoken, well groomed, self-assured, and well mannered.

On the baseball diamond, however, Monte Ward was a fireball. Since in his day the captain of a baseball nine was really the manager, Monte, as field captain, ran the ball club. He tolerated no loafing on the field, no drunkards, no goof-offs. Because he himself devoted every ounce of his strength and speed and attention to the game, he demanded exactly that from all his mates. He would bawl out those who failed him, big as they might be, in a manner befitting a drill sergeant — often with language so hair-raising that on occasion even the toughest of them was taken aback. (And had any of Monte's society friends ever heard his tirades, they'd have very likely fallen in a faint.) But none of his teammates ever resented Monte Ward, for he was fair and honest in all his dealings with them. He stood up for the ballplayer against the owner in all arguments and he played his heart out in every game.

Ward began as a pitcher, straight out of college, with the Providence club of the National League. He was eighteen years old then but had already grown to full strength. He had a smoking fastball and a good curve and used them both to win 22 games out of the 35 he pitched in his first season, 1878. Next season, under manager George Wright (Harry Wright's kid brother), Monte helped George consistently beat Harry's Boston Reds and claim the pennant by winning 47 games out of 63 he pitched. The year after that, 1880, five days after a pitcher from Brown University, Lee Richmond, pitched the first "perfect" game ever recorded in the league, Monte pitched the second one. In nine innings against Buffalo, Ward allowed no hits and no runs, and allowed no man to reach base. Monte also won 39 more games that season.

It is no wonder that, despite his youth, his strength, and his excellent condition, Monte Ward soon developed a sore arm. In his five seasons with Providence he hurled 215 complete games, besides playing third base and outfield when not pitching. In his final two seasons, Ward put in more and more time as an outfielder and began to play shortstop as well — an ideal position for him, one in which he could take charge in the infield, advise the pitcher, and make use of his strong arm.

NATIONAL BASEBALL HALL OF FAME

Monte after joining the New York club

In 1883 Ward joined the New York club, as pitcher, third baseman, second baseman, shortstop, and outfielder. He soon settled at shortstop and won his greatest fame there. As shortstop, with no need to fret over his sore pitching arm, Ward's batting improved sharply — and he had always been a swift and aggressive base runner. He developed into the acknowledged leader of the club, the fellow who could drive even the slowest of players into frenzies of effort. He knew every aspect of the game by this time and could pick out a batter's or a fielder's flaws quickly and explain them accurately — and sometimes bitterly. When his Giants beat out the Brooklyn club of the American Association for the championship, it was agreed that Monte Ward's profane and scalding locker room recitation of the sins of his pitchers was the goad that woke up the whole club and inspired them to win.

There may have been players who resented Ward's smooth and wicked tongue. But when it came time to choose a man to lead the Players' Brotherhood in the struggle to win a better deal from the club owners, the players knew there was no better man than Ward. Ward's opponent in this struggle was another smooth talker — Al Spalding, a far more devious man and one not given to putting any trust whatsoever in his fellow creatures.

Spalding invited Ward in 1887 to attend the annual league meeting as a representative of the players. The item the players most wanted to complain about was the strict limitation of salaries to two thousand dollars a year. (The limitation was secretly violated in deals with some of the top players.) At the meeting, Spalding and the other club owners gave Ward their assurance that "differences would be adjusted," whereupon Spalding set off on a great Australian baseball tour that proved so successful it expanded into a trip around the world. Ward was invited, along with other great stars like Cap Anson and Ned Williamson, Chicago's home-run hitter.

The traveling team played baseball not only in Australia, but in Ceylon, Italy, France, England, Ireland, and even in the shadow of the Egyptian pyramids. When Ward came home, however, he found that the club owners — undoubtedly with Spalding's full knowledge — had been playing games of their own: they had worked out a scheme, called a "classification rule," that froze salaries throughout the league, making it impossible for a player on a team in the lowest standing ever to make more than a tiny wage. This was so much worse a deal than the original salary limitation that the players, almost without exception, flew into a rage. Ward called upon Spalding to arrange an immediate conference with the club owners, but Spalding responded that there was "nothing to discuss" and that any complaint could be taken up at the regular meeting in the fall.

The Brotherhood members would not wait; they set out immediately to create a new league — to be run by the players themselves. With almost every famous name in the league ready to walk out and join a new league, it was relatively easy to find investors who would finance the new clubs. When the 1890 season began there was a new major league, the Players' League, filled with all the great stars from the National League.

Monte Ward became manager of the new club in Brooklyn, where he played shortstop, batted .337, and stole sixty-three bases. The National League tottered on the verge of bankruptcy while putting out false attendance figures — which friendly newspapers dutifully reported — to make it look as if the league was doing well. The Players' League did not do much better, playing in makeshift parks and facing scorn from most of the major sportswriters. (Even thirty years later, one sports reporter wrote that the Players' League had been a "bolshevik organization.") By playing off one owner against another, offering fat inducements one day and quickly withdrawing them the next, Spalding and his allies soon had the Players' League backers frightened into selling out one by one, and the players' whole scheme eventually collapsed. But at least for many years afterward, the National League club owners (who did not relish another brush with bankruptcy) were quick to make concessions if there was even a whisper of a new "Brotherhood."

Monte Ward stayed in Brooklyn, as manager–second baseman of the National League club, and in 1893 returned to the Giants, where he batted .348 and stole forty-six bases. (With Brooklyn, the year before, he had stolen eighty-eight.) He was still the most popular man on the team — still adored by the fans and still admired by his teammates.

The new owner of the Giants was Andrew Freedman, a testy, egotistical man who wanted his own way in all things. Even though Monte Ward, in two seasons as manager, lifted the Giants from fifth place to second, Freedman fired him outright. Monte, still under thirty-five years old, batting .265, and stealing bases at a good clip, left the diamond for good.

He had written a book about baseball, the first ever written by a professional player — and, unlike the many ghostwritten books by others that followed, it was actually written by the athlete himself. Today's readers would find much to smile at in Ward's book, *Baseball: How to Become a Player*. Ward, who himself often enjoyed a polite highball at a midtown bar, warned his young readers to avoid all strong drink. However, a glass of ale, beer, or claret with meals, he said, was "in some cases beneficial," especially if a young fellow was thin and nervous.

And Monte had fault to find with some of the "modern" trends of his day. The idea of asking a catcher to give signals to the pitcher was ridiculous, he wrote, because a catcher "has enough of his own to attend to." Anyway, he pointed out, only one signal was ever needed: if the pitch was not a fastball, it would be a curve. (A few years later, writers had everyone believing that pitchers could curve the ball both ways on the same pitch, make it jump before it reached the plate, or actually curve it back toward the pitcher.)

Perhaps recalling how his own mighty arm had given out from trying to throw full strength every day, Monte urged young pitchers to avoid relying on "brute strength" and to turn instead to craft and the careful conserving of strength. If a game was safely won, said Monte, the pitcher might well resort to tossing the ball in underhand, so as not to tire himself too soon. (Nowadays, a pitcher who fails to "throw strikes" when he has a comfortable lead is likely to hear a long recital of his sins from the manager.)

Monte Ward wrote no more books after he left baseball. Instead, he set himself up in the practice of law and very soon became one of the wealthiest lawyers in New York City. He retained his interest in baseball and some years later bought himself a half-interest in the Boston club of the National League. But he sold out his share before the season was over: he just did not feel comfortable sitting on the other side of the fence from the boys he had led to battle twenty-five years before.

CHARLES COMISKEY

Father of the American League

The name *Comiskey* has survived only as the designation of an old ball park in Chicago, but for a long time it was one of the most renowned in sports — the name of the game's greatest first baseman, manager and promoter, an innovator who made radical changes in playing technique, helped build a brand-new major league all by himself, and created in Chicago what in its time was the finest baseball field in the world. Charles Comiskey — Commy — opened up infield play, added untold speed and aggressiveness to the game, forced the authorities to draw lines around the coaching areas to keep him from roaming up and down the baselines when his club was at bat, taught the pitcher to cover first base, and spread the gospel of catering to the comfort and enjoyment of the people who paid to see ball games. (He also exhibited a reactionary trend when he refused to let Western Union telegraphers send out inning-by-inning reports on his games: "They're stealing my ball games!" he insisted.)

Comiskey won his early reputation in Saint Louis, as first baseman–

manager of the Saint Louis Browns. There he not only demonstrated his skill at playing far off the base, but showed unusual talent at sizing up and recruiting ballplayers. He built the Saint Louis Browns into champions, saw his boss trade away many of the best players, and built up another team of winners with players recruited from far and near.

Commy, the son of a prosperous brickyard owner, began playing baseball in his hometown of Chicago. He was shipped off to school to keep him from "wasting" his boyhood playing baseball. But he played ball anyway, and when he was sent on to Saint Mary's College in Kansas, he became captain of the freshman baseball team. At Saint Mary's he met the man whom he always credited with teaching him how to improve his play and how to run a baseball club — Timothy P. "Ted" Sullivan, who became one of the most noted organizers in professional baseball. (His name lived longest, however, in connection with the "Sullivan sleepers" — the day coaches in which his baseball teams made their all-night journeys.) Ted, shortstop and pitcher on the college nine, turned Commy from an outfielder into a catcher, a job Ted decided Commy had earned because he was "the smartest kid on the team."

Commy was removed from Saint Mary's College, however, and was sent to Christian Brothers College at Prairie du Chien, Wisconsin, where no time was allowed for baseball. But in the summer he rejoined Ted Sullivan in Milwaukee, playing for one of the "make-believe amateur" nines called the Alerts. Here Commy, for the first time in his life, received money for playing baseball — fifty dollars a month "expenses" from the Alerts. He became a pitcher, but the team's catchers (barehanded in that day) complained that he threw the ball too hard and was hashing up their fingers. So Commy moved next spring to Elgin, Illinois, to play for the Elgin Watch team, and there he found a catcher named Rudy Kemmler who was not afraid of Commy's pitching speed. Together they won every game the Elgin Watch team played.

In 1878, Ted Sullivan invited Commy to come to Dubuque, Iowa, where Ted operated a news agency and where he planned to establish a professional baseball league. Commy, as pitcher and utility man, received fifty dollars a month during the season and in the off-season he sold newspapers and magazines on commission. Commy, in Dubuque, developed a big "outcurve" — a sure get-them-out pitch in that era — and led Dubuque to the championship of the Northwestern League, which had been put together by Sullivan with teams from Dubuque, Omaha, Rockford, and Davenport. This was the first minor league ever created and it employed a number of ballplayers who later earned fame in the National League. Despite sharp competition and fine play, the league lost a bundle of cash and Ted folded it after one season. He hung on to his Dubuque Rabbits, however, and turned them into a traveling team who would go most anywhere to find a decent gate.

The Rabbits did so well on the road that they were invited to play an exhibition against the famed Saint Louis Browns, run by a voluble beer-garden owner named Chris von der Ahe (which Chris pronounced, at the top of his lungs, "Aw!"). Al Spink, a former Canadian who, with his brother Charles, eventually founded *The Sporting News,* was very impressed with Commy's performance at first base during the Browns game. (Commy's pitching arm had begun to come up sore, so he was playing from time to time almost every position on the team.)

Al Spink wrote Commy a letter after the game inviting him to come join the Browns, who were paying, said Al, "from $90 to $125 a month." Commy had just gotten married and ached to move on to bigger things, but he would not move until he had received permission from Ted. Ted allowed that Commy was too good for his club anyway and he urged him to take the offer. Commy became a Brown, but not without an argument. When he got to Saint Louis, von der Ahe wanted him to play right field. No, said Commy, it was first base or he'd go back home. The boss gave in, Commy played first, and within a month von der Ahe had raised his salary to $150. Commy was an immediate hit with the Saint Louis fans, who yelled and yelled the first time Commy ventured into short right field from his first base position to catch a fly (this was the first time they had seen such a deed performed on any ball field in town). Even the greatest of first basemen in that time held their jobs mostly because of their bats — they confined their "fielding" to catching hard throws from the other players. Players like Cap Anson and Joe Start and Roger Connor and Dan Brouthers felt no urge to venture off toward second base into foreign territory, and they would not have dreamed of poaching on the right fielder's ground. Many a wiseacre who saw Commy playing out on the grass declared his whole performance "unnatural," and they predicted chaos as soon as a hot grounder came out Commy's way while he left first base uncovered. A hot grounder did come down toward first base one day and Commy gobbled it up a long way beyond the bag. The bleacher bugs all exchanged an "I-told-you-so" look and waited to see Commy scramble helplessly while the runner coasted in to first laughing. But lo and behold, Commy just flipped the ball to the base — and there was the pitcher, of all people, ready to take the throw and make the out. The Saint Louis fans simply howled in delight. Who in the world taught the pitcher to make a play like that?

Well, Commy taught him — just as he taught the shortstop to move to cover second base or third when the baseman had business elsewhere. Commy's team was always moving, backing each other up, looking for chances to get into the play — no matter where the ball was hit. There had been, since the days of Dickey Pearce, infielders who shifted about with the change of batters, or who played inside or outside the baseline, depending on the situation. But no club had ever moved about in such a coordinated manner as Commy's boys did. No wonder Chris von der Ahe swelled up with pride and named apartment houses after his Brownies! And no wonder the Saint Louis fans took the team, and particularly Charles Comiskey, to their bosoms.

It was inevitable that Commy took over the captaincy — that is, managership — of the Browns and schooled the whole gang in combination plays. To watch a team like this, one that kept shifting about with the precision of a machine, was a truly exciting spectacle to fans who had been brought up on the old-fashioned stationary type of play. The stands were always full. Von der Ahe sold barrels and barrels of beer (hawked throughout the stands by aproned and mustachioed vendors who carried a bouquet of flowing steins in each fist and shouted, "Give your orders, gents!"). And the Browns showed fat profits at the gate. They even traveled to New York for a championship game one fall in a special train with Brownie banners festooning every car.

Von der Ahe, who fancied himself a genius in the baseball business, observed that his rival genius — A. G. Spalding of the Chicago White Stockings, whose team his Browns had beaten several times — had been able to get $10,000 in exchange for his star, Mike Kelly, and another $10,000 for his best pitcher, John Clarkson. So von der Ahe decided to fatten his own purse that way and proceeded to sell some of the men who had won him the league championship in 1885 and 1886. After the Browns had won their third pennant, in 1887, without even mentioning the deals to Comiskey, von der Ahe sold his top pitcher, Bob Carruthers, and his second best, Dave Foutz, along with "Doc" Bushong, his number-one catcher, to Brooklyn, for $10,000. Then he sent Curt Welch, star outfielder and hero of the 1886 winner-take-all game with the White Stockings, to Philadelphia, along with shortstop Bill Gleason, for $5,000. This tore the guts out of the championship club and left Comiskey without any shortstop at all.

The Saint Louis fans — and Comiskey, too — were in a mood to hang Chris von der Ahe to a lamppost. But von der Ahe soothed Commy's feelings by giving him a raise that nourished his bankroll, and Comiskey set out to build a new team around the wreck of the old. He recruited veterans and newcomers from all over the civilized world — or at least that part of it between the Mississippi River and the Atlantic Ocean — and started immediately to win ball games again. He took the pennant in 1888 and led the club to New York to tackle the Gotham Giants. He lost that game, but the Browns made their usual spectacular show as they crossed the country in their banner-bedecked special train, and old Chris had no fears for the future.

But even Commy's inspired direction could not bring the Browns in first again, for the men von der Ahe had traded ganged up to help knock the Saint Louis team out of the top spot in the American Association. After that came the Brotherhood strike, in which Commy, like Mike Kelly, stuck with the boys. Commy came back to Saint Louis after the strike, and he led the league in putouts in 1891. But the club came in second again and attendance at the games was meager. There had been just too much shuffling of ballplayers: the loyalties of the local fans had faded. Besides, the American Association itself had begun to totter and eventually it had to merge with the National League, to make a twelve-team organization. A. G. Spalding had invited Commy to move to Chicago and run a second Chicago ball club in the park where the Brotherhood team had been playing. (Spalding at the time owned the park.) But Commy had no capital and Spalding would not supply it. Instead, with the outlook so dismal in Saint Louis, Commy took a job as field leader of the Cincinnati club.

In Cincinnati, Commy accomplished no miracles. But he did himself a great deal of good when he found a drinking and card-playing companion in a chubby young sportswriter named Byron Bancroft "Ban" Johnson. Commy landed Ban Johnson a job as president of the Western League. Then he joined Johnson in the league, taking over the Sioux City, Iowa, franchise and moving it to Saint Paul.

The two young men shared the same dream — a new major league, rooted in the Midwest, to compete with and maybe even completely demolish the National League. Commy had no respect at all for the National League club owners. After his experience in the Brotherhood strike, he considered them all a bunch of phonies — double-dealers, liars, con men, and cowards. When his Cincinnati boss, Garry Herrmann, came back from a league meeting and discovered he had lost his watch, Commy snorted. "What did you expect?" said Commy. "Look at the gang you were with!"

Johnson and Comiskey were not cowards. If they had been, they'd have dumped the Western League after one season of struggle and frustration. But they kept trying, bringing in new club owners to pump fresh blood into the league, and hastening to patch up leaks wherever they showed. Eventually they turned it into a major league and set out to invade National League territory — not just in Chicago, but in the big eastern cities as well. They would change their name to the American League and either fight the National League or cooperate with it — whichever the older league might choose. And their first moves would be to get out of Saint Paul and Grand Rapids and move into Chicago and Cleveland.

Spalding and his cohorts decided it would be no great task to wipe this upstart minor league right off the map. They let Commy have the decaying park down by the stockyards — where they were sure the odors from the yards would drive fans away — and secured an agreement guaranteeing that the new team would not identify itself as a Chicago club and that Spalding could draft one player each year from Commy's roster. Commy got around the name restriction by naming the team the White Sox. Everyone knew the White Stockings (a name long since abandoned by the National League club) had belonged to Chicago. So there was no need for any further identification.

Commy had learned in Saint Louis that fans would turn out almost anywhere for twenty-five-cent baseball, so he set that price for his bleacher seats — and he filled the park, bush-league lineup or not. He soon improved his lineup, too, for Ban Johnson's efforts to secure peaceful cooperation from the National League were unsuccessful, and the new league began to raid the rosters of the old league.

Commy was growing fat from sitting too much in office chairs and knew he could no longer perform on the field. So he hired a National League pitcher, Clark Griffith — who for six seasons had won more than twenty games a season for the Chicago National League club — to manage and pitch for the White Sox. Griffith won twenty-four games his first season.

Commy now retreated to the office and did no more field managing, even though there were times when he felt he knew more about what tactics were needed than the field manager did. But he recalled from his own active days that it did not pay to second-guess a manager.

Commy's first concern now was the cultivation of the fans. There was no way to restore the Brotherhood park, so Commy bought a new spot, just a few hundred feet away, and built the finest ball park of its time. (Spalding's competing National League park had been one of the wonders of the world when it was created some years before.) Commy's park had concrete and steel grandstands, with an "ornamental brick wall" all around and more cheap bleacher seats (twenty-five cents) than any other park in either league. It held 28,500 fans altogether, and within a very few seasons had to make room for 3,500 more. (Eventually it was expanded to hold about 50,000.)

Commy, like a number of ex-players who became club owners, was exceedingly "thrifty" (a polite word for stingy) when it came to players' salaries. But he was generosity itself toward the fans and toward his baseball friends. The park, he maintained, really belonged to the fans, and whenever any group of them wanted to use the place — for a picnic, a rally, a track meet, or no matter what — Commy turned it over for free. "I like to see people enjoy themselves," he would say.

He formed an organization for his friends called the Woodland Bards and occasionally took them all to his hunting lodge — where there was more hilarity than hunting. To this day in the White Sox park there is a Bards' Room where food and drink are served — but no longer for free. For himself, Commy built a little cage right under the stands so he could keep a close eye on proceedings without seeming to interfere. He grew wider and heavier each year and wore a wide-brimmed hat that gave him the appearance of a senator or an itinerant preacher. He was called the Old Roman now, and became a sort of father figure in the game. The changes he had made in baseball and, above all, his burning desire to come in first were reflected in the traditions of the White Sox through succeeding decades.

It was Commy who instilled the desire for speed, for constant action, for tight infield play. No player on any of Commy's teams was ever allowed to stand by and watch. If there was nothing going on in his vicinity, he could just as well get over *fast* and back up a throw or cover an empty base. And in Commy's mind there was never any such thing

NATIONAL BASEBALL HALL OF FAME

Commy — "the Old Roman"

as a game that was safely won or hopelessly lost. If he had a ten-run lead he wanted more and more. Once, when an umpire called a game because of darkness, with Commy's club sixteen runs behind, Commy roared a protest. The umpire waved him down.

"Did you really think you had a chance to *win* this?" asked the umpire.

"Not after you called it, we didn't," growled Commy.

Perhaps the lowest point in Commy's career came with the revelation that his 1919 pennant winners had thrown the World Series to the Cincinnati Reds. When the favored Sox lost the series, Commy took note of the gossip concerning the comings and goings of gamblers and the strange fluctuations in the betting odds. By this time, Ban Johnson, president of the league, and Commy — the former drinking buddies — were full-time enemies and not speaking to each other. So Commy asked the president of the other league, William Heydler, to make an investigation of the rumors of World Series fraud. Johnson talked Heydler out of it. "That's just the yelp of the beaten cur!" said Ban about Commy's complaint.

But Hugh Fullerton, a Chicago sportswriter, brought the gossip into the open and Commy promptly offered a reward of $10,000 if anyone could prove the series had not been played on the level. (Some players did say that if Commy had spread that money among his own miserably paid hired hands, they'd never have had to sell out to gamblers.) An angry letter to a newspaper (actually written by one of the paper's own reporters) finally started a grand-jury investigation, and with that many of the players grew uneasy.

Eddie Cicotte, the star Chicago pitcher, rushed to Commy's office to confess his part in the misdeeds. "Don't tell me about it," Commy said. "Tell the grand jury." And Cicotte did, reciting a tale of money slipped under his pillow, of double-crosses and crude throwing of games. Other players talked freely to newswriters of the way the games were dumped. But by the time the matter finally came to trial, incriminating records had vanished; the players repudiated their confessions, lawyers from the district attorney's office appeared as counsel for the defense, and the jury brought in not-guilty verdicts for all. The jury and the players then went out together and celebrated until long past midnight.

But the players were still guilty in Commy's mind, as they were in the baseball commissioner's. Commy vowed that none of them would ever play for the White Sox again. And the newly appointed commissioner, Judge Kenesaw Mountain Landis, made it official by barring the whole gang from organized baseball forever. Nobody ever earned the $10,000 reward—which (although they had promised much more) was exactly equal to the amount the gamblers had paid out to the players.

LEWIS ROGERS (PETE) BROWNING

The Original Louisville Slugger

Pete Browning did not actually invent the Louisville Slugger bat, but he was the man for whom the first such bat was made. A woodturner in Louisville named John Hillerich turned out the bat to Pete's specifications in the summer of 1884 and very soon found himself in the bat business — other ballplayers decided they needed to own a made-to-order weapon, just as Peter Browning did. The firm of Hillerich & Bradby still makes bats for the big leagues, to suit batters of every size and strength. Before Pete had his bat made (and Pete owned seven hundred of them) bats were often ordered wholesale by the club management and each player had to saw or whittle his down to suit himself.

There probably never was a ballplayer in the leagues who loved to hit any more than Pete Browning did. Hitting was all he cared for, talked about, or bragged about. He played nearly every position in baseball at the beginning of his career — he even pitched part of an inning in one game, allowing two hits and retiring one batter. But eventually he

NATIONAL BASEBALL HALL OF FAME

Pete Browning sporting Louisville uniform and his renowned mustache

settled in the outfield, possibly because that was where he could do his team the least harm as a fielder. Pete disliked contact. He had a horror of getting hit by a ball, and he became adept at squirming and dodging at the plate to avoid pitches without yielding the spot into which he had dug himself. On base, he simply refused to slide. And in the outfield he would take special care not to overexert himself, catch cold, or get chilblains.

Pete had a chronic abscess in one ear that partially deafened him. That may have been one of the reasons why he so feared being hit or bumped into. His deafness made it necessary for his friends to raise their voices when they spoke to him. And Pete must have thought everyone had the same trouble, for he always talked at the top of his lungs, announcing his readiness to collect loads of base hits and run like a deer around the bases. He enjoyed talking matters over with the fans in the bleachers when he took the field and happily kept them all informed about the state of his health: "The old dogs are fine!" he would tell them. "The old lamps are full of base hits!" His feet (dogs) and his eyes (lamps) and his bats — those were the things Pete fretted most about and took the most tender care of. He would never get his feet wet. And he used to sand and polish and caress his bats as if they were live animals that had to be curried to keep them looking sleek. As for his eyes, he imagined he was keeping them in prime shape by never getting soap and water anywhere near them. When he washed his face, he took extra care to keep the suds far from his eyes. And if the sun was shining, he would start the day by trotting outside and staring right up at the sun. That, he felt, was the sure way to keep his eyes bright and sharp. (It was a miracle he did not make himself blind as well as deaf.)

Pete was a big man — six feet tall, in that era when six-footers were rare. But he carried no extra weight, was swift as a pony on the bases, and had shoulders like a coal heaver. When he promised the world that he had a carload of base hits to deliver, he made good on his promise. He came into the big leagues with Louisville of the American Association and in his first season led the league, with a .378 batting average. For seven seasons in a row he hit better than .300 and one season (1887) hit .402. It was no wonder he was the most popular man in town, followed everywhere he went by a happy crowd of admirers, to whom he called out greetings in a voice that made windowpanes tremble. Pete had an enormous mustache that gave him the look of a happy walrus. His face always shone as if it had been polished, and his eyes were everlastingly a-gleam. Like a number of other athletic heroes, he took to talking about himself in the third person. Because of his dauntless way with pitchers over the seasons, he finally earned the title "Old Gladiator." He shortened that to "Gladdy" and would often announce to his fans: "Old Gladdy's going to line them out today!"

Pete believed in conditioning. Fond as he was of rich, greasy food — and though he was even fonder of "German tea" (his pet name for beer) — Pete denied himself both all through the winter so he could show up in the spring lean and alert. The only trouble with his system was that once the baseball season had begun his training rules were abandoned and he indulged himself as often as he was tempted. And with hundreds of fans eager to treat him to one or two or even a dozen steins of German tea, and with groups of every size urging him to attend their dinners, Pete's physical condition grew steadily worse as the season grew older. Still, Pete's batting average stayed high, except for the season of 1889, just before the Brotherhood strike, when for the first time in his major-league career his batting average fell below .300.

In the Players' League, in 1890, Pete was once more at the top of the list, with an official batting average of .373. Whether this figure agreed with Pete's own figure, no one knows; Pete used to work out his own average regularly throughout the season, sweating over the arithmetic for many minutes a day before happily broadcasting the figure — if it turned out to suit him. "Old Pete is hitting .395!" he would shout, even to those who had no interest in such matters.

Pete Browning never had any enemies, or at least he never *wanted* to make any. He irritated many people by his manner of play, especially by his haphazard fielding. But he was always penitent if he hurt anyone's feelings or did another man an injury. He even apologized once for hitting a home run. His manager had ordered him to bunt, and a fan in the nearby cheap seats screamed: "Put 'er in the canal, Pete!" Instinctively, Pete hauled off and belted the ball clean over the fence. It did not quite make it to the water, but it did land in a backyard, where an innocent lady, hanging out her wash, nearly jumped over the clothesline in fright. When Pete had completed his trip around the bases, he approached the bench with both hands held up placatingly toward the manager. "I know! I know," said Pete. "But that damn bug in the bleachers got me rattled!"

Pete also could be rattled by being called upon to make a speech. Despite his ingrained habit of orating to his beloved fans in the bleachers, he would grow tongue-tied if he had to stand up at a formal occasion and acknowledge the fans' devotion. In 1887, when he attained the highest batting average of his career, Pete's Louisville fans chipped in and bought him one of those "turnip" watches so popular with wealthy men of that day—heavy gold, about the size of a snowball, with Pete's initials, *LRB,* in scroll script on the case. (Pete's 1887 average is now given as .402, but actually it was listed then as .471, because bases on balls were counted as hits that season; modern statisticians have revised the 1887 average by throwing out the bases on balls.) The fans arranged a banquet for Pete, loaded him with praise, then presented the watch. Pete was truly made speechless. His red face glowing even redder than usual, he stood and looked lovingly at the regal gift. "Speech! Speech!" the diners yelled. "Speak up, Pete!"

Finally, after swallowing a few times, Pete managed to blurt: "Where the hell's the chain?" This really shattered his eager listeners, who pounded the table in delight.

Merry times like this were what led to the falling off of old Pete's batting average in 1889. Indeed, in that year he once showed up for a game with so much beer aboard that he was not fit to take his place on the diamond. For this he was fined six hundred dollars — a very large chunk of his salary. But it wasn't the loss of the money that scared Pete — it was the loss of his licks at bat. He immediately "took the pledge" and went all that season and the next without tasting German tea even once.

But after the Players' League folded up, Pete, who had been playing in Cleveland, was signed by Pittsburgh in the National League, and after fifty games there he was traded to Cincinnati. In that city, where German tea flowed like water in half a hundred beer gardens, Pete found two merry companions of similar tastes, pitcher Billy Rhines and catcher Jerry Harrington. Together, this unholy trinity began to make a regular circuit of the beer gardens every summer night. Cincinnati seemed like paradise to Pete.

After carefully studying the bats of all the rival hitters who came to town, Pete bought himself a hundred new bats — a copy of every one that looked and felt good to him. He boosted his batting average to back over .300, and he must have assured himself and his friends a hundred times that old Pete was going to smack three hits every day.

But Pete's carousing was too much for manager Tom Loftus to bear and he turned Pete loose to wander back to Louisville. Back home, the Old Gladiator began to fail at the plate. The following season, 1893, he batted well over .300 again, but he was in such poor shape he could play in only fifty-seven games — so even the local management wanted no more of Pete.

Pete managed to arrange brief tryouts with Saint Louis and Brooklyn, but he played in only two games with the former team and one with the latter. Pete found himself a job then in Allentown, Pennsylvania, where King Kelly was playing his final few games of baseball and trying to prove he could manage a ball club. Pete stayed with Allentown until one day when he had to run back after a long fly ball. A huge puddle had formed in the outfield of the primitive ball park and the water hazard stretched right between Pete Browning and the spot where the ball was heading. Did the Old Gladiator run through the deep puddle in his baseball shoes and risk contracting some crippling ailment in the old dogs for the team's sake? Not Old Gladdy! He pulled up short on the shore of the puddle and watched the ball go bouncing away.

King Kelly, seeing such cowardice — not to say plain treachery — said a number of bad words out loud. And when Pete came in to the bench, Mike notified him he was fired.

Pete took this setback calmly and did not let it diminish his self-confidence by even half an ounce. Old Gladdy would just go back to Louisville, he told himself, where there was sure to be a job awaiting. As for Kelly — well, Pete told his friends at home, "The old fool was just jealous because I hit more home runs than he did."

Pete did find a job, or at least a chance to play ball for a few dollars with a semipro club. But he spent a lot of time, too, haunting the major-league park to interview visiting managers in hopes of finding a place on their rosters.

"Look at them lamps!" he would urge them. "Just full of sunshine and full of base hits!" But nobody would take a chance with Pete anymore. So the seasons rolled by. The old lamps began to dim and the old dogs grew weary.

Finally, in a desperate effort to stay in the big league, Pete called on league president Nick Young and begged for a job as umpire — then a low-paying position without much honor (the league was always reluctant to back up an umpire in a dispute with a tough manager). But Young just could not bring himself to hire a man like Pete, a famous night-rounder and a professional good fellow, to try to keep a ball game in control. Besides, the man was sick.

Pete's health indeed had begun to fail. His ear abscess, which had never been cured, grew critical now and the doctor ordered an operation. Poor old Pete, just a shadow of his once strong and fleet-footed self, died after the operation, at the age of forty-seven.

CORNELIUS McGILLICUDDY

The Indestructible Connie Mack

Cornelius McGillicuddy never knew the time when he was not called Connie Mack. When he first became aware of the world around him, in East Brookfield, Massachusetts, in 1862, his family was known to neighbors as "the Macks" — not because the neighbors knew no better but simply because it was too much trouble to recite all the syllables when speaking about the McGillicuddys. And it was that way in other spots in America where folks from McGillicuddy Reeks, in Ireland, had settled.

The Macks were a poor family in the 1860s and 1870s, when times were hard — as they always are for the poor. At the age of ten, Cornelius, the third child, was working, during school vacations, a twelve-hour day, six days a week, in a local cotton mill. Once he had finished grammar school he took a full-time job in a shoe factory nearby. Yet he did find time to play ball — not real baseball, like today's game, but some of the other forms that were still being played in the New England countryside, even when the New York game had become the

BOSTON PUBLIC LIBRARY, PRINT DEPARTMENT, MCGREEVEY COLLECTION

Connie Mack

style in most of the big eastern cities. Connie played round ball, sting ball, and one-hole cat in the open spaces around home. And on big holidays, when boys would crowd into town from all the local farms, he might get into a game of town ball, with thirty boys on a side, each yelling his little lungs out.

By the time Connie had got his growth, the New York game had been adopted everywhere and there was hardly a small town in the state that did not father a baseball team of some sort — with uniforms and regular bats and balls. The larger cities, like Worcester, Hartford (Connecticut), Boston, and Fall River, all had leagues of their own with a dozen or so amateur clubs competing for a "championship." Small-town teams would range widely about their part of the state, in horse-drawn wagons or in trolleys or even in railroad steam cars, to meet rival teams, all organized in a "league" of sorts.

Connie, called "Slats" by his playmates, had grown exceptionally tall by the time he was in his teens. He was spare as a scarecrow — all arms and legs and joints — and could apparently reach out and snag any ball that came within twenty feet of his hand. He early joined the East Brookfield nine of the Central Massachusetts Amateur League as catcher and he worked chiefly as a catcher throughout his playing career. But he would never have thought of baseball as a way to earn money if times had not grown harder still. He lost his job in the factory when he was twenty-two years old, and took a job at ninety dollars a month playing ball for Meriden of the Connecticut State League. From that time on he stayed in professional baseball until he was almost ninety.

At Meriden, Connie never startled anyone with his power at the plate or even with exceptional fielding skill. But he did develop some tricks that increased his effectiveness as a catcher and helped his club win a lot of ball games. He had always been a boy who loved to talk — never in a loud and vulgar manner, but gently, interminably, in a soft, squeaky voice that could drive a batter nuts. He had early in life developed great talent at detecting just what subject, or what phrases, were best designed to get under another person's skin. Behind the plate, he would gently ask each batter questions bound to embarrass or annoy him — about his appearance, his dress, his recent behavior, or his last major mistake — until the batter's neck would begin to burn and he could barely keep his mind on the pitch.

Connie also learned very early how to smack his hands together to make a sound like a ball skipping off the bat. Wearing only the small fingerless gloves that catchers used in that era, he could make that "foul-tip" noise without the umpire ever seeing how he did it. Then he would grab the ball on the fly and — in keeping with the then-current rule that "a tick and a 'ketch' will always fetch" — would have the batter out. Very soon the rule was changed, preventing this practice except on strike three. But Connie always had a new trick to bedevil batters with, and he was smart in other ways, too — an ideal catcher really, for he knew how to place the fielders, having begun early in life to study the habits of batters until he could tell you in advance exactly where each man's hits were most likely to fall. His arm was strong and he could get rid of a ball so fast it often seemed as if he had started to throw before he received the pitch. He was also gifted at gentling any pitcher who had begun to lose his cool: his soft voice and easy flow of words were balm to a man who was getting rattled.

His strong arm and his smartness, plus his flow of words, soon earned Connie a better job, with Hartford, where he was teamed with a pitcher just as lanky and lean as he was — Frank Gilmore. Together they became known as the "Bones Battery" and were easily the best in the league. When the Connecticut State League season closed, Connie made himself a few extra dollars by catching in some games for the New York Metropolitans — the original Mets — an American Association club that shared a park with the New York Giants.

Next season Frank Gilmore received a big-league offer from the Washington club of the National League, but he refused to move unless he could bring his battery mate with him. So the Bones Battery moved to Washington together and became known as the "Hartford Battery." Fans used to crowd the park to watch them. Not that they won many ball games — but it was worth the price of admission to see those two long, angular creatures jumping about like grasshoppers while keeping the game alive with endless chatter.

Connie by this time had begun to play other positions on the diamond — as most of the old-time players did, since rosters were small and budgets stingy. He played second base and outfield in his second year with Washington and before he was through he had done time at shortstop and both first and second bases. When Connie started off in the major league it looked as if he had suddenly developed into a slugger, for he achieved a batting average of .361 (in ten games). Playing a full schedule the following season, Connie lost ground at bat. His average in 1887 dropped to .201, and the next season it was .187. He got adjusted to big-league pitching after that and kept his average well over .200. In his entire eleven-year active career, Connie hit only five home runs. By 1893, when batting averages in general began to improve because the pitching distance was lengthened from fifty feet to sixty feet, six inches, Connie had retired from active play.

After the 1889 season, Connie went on strike, as did most of the other top players in the two established leagues; he joined the newly formed Players' League and played the season of 1890 as catcher and part owner of the Buffalo club. He caught in nearly every game, setting a single-season record of 119 games as catcher that stood until 1902 — and his record might have stood forever if the Players' League had been able to remain alive to complete the 1890 season. But as it turned out, the league began to crumble; the Buffalo players worked the latter part of their abbreviated season for nothing. In Connie's case it was for less than nothing, for he saw all his savings vanish with the collapse of the league.

When the returning players were sorted out after the end of the Brotherhood strike, Connie Mack was awarded to Pittsburgh in the National League and he resumed his career as the "talking catcher." New rules made it far easier for Connie to talk now, for the catcher was required to move up behind the plate and catch while tucked in a spot right under the bat. This put a final end to Connie's trick of faking foul tips, for there was no room to perform his stunt and still catch the ball. So he worked out a new trick, one well suited to the new position: he used to reach up as a batter started his swing and gently tip the end of the bat, causing it to veer suddenly off course and miss the ball by a foot. Connie always expressed his deep regret at such an accident. But finally one victim grew tired of accepting apologies in place of base hits and took dead aim next time at bat — not at the ball but at Connie's hands. He managed to mash the tricky catcher's fingers so vigorously that Connie was out of action for several days.

Connie was injured again while catching in Pittsburgh in 1894 and had to spend weeks on the bench. This was in a day when catchers had no Safety Guard chest protectors and wore no shin guards (or if they did, they kept them hidden under their stockings). Naked of padded armor, long-legged Connie crouched in front of the plate, ball in hand, to put a tag on Boston's Herman Long, a solid little man who was entirely unaccustomed to fear. Long hit Connie at top speed, which for him was much faster than most other men on the field. Although Connie was six inches taller than Long, he was about ten pounds lighter. In the collison, Connie suffered a broken ankle and a torn leg muscle. But Long, too, failed to get up after the collision and was himself laid low for many weeks.

After that injury, Connie was never again able to crouch comfortably behind the plate and had to leave one long, skinny leg outstretched. This greatly limited his mobility. He was only twenty-eight, but he could see the end of his playing career not far ahead. Before the season of 1894 was over he was offered a chance to run the club and he accepted happily. He began at once to cut down on his own playing time. In 1895, he played but thirteen games, one of them at first base. The following year he played first base practically all the time, before quitting the Pittsburgh team at the end of the season.

Connie by this time had got wind of Byron Bancroft Johnson's scheme for turning the Western League into a third major league, and he moved west to manage the Milwaukee club. On this job Connie first met the wild Dutchman who was to become one of his greatest stars — George Edward Waddell, who eventually became famous as "Rube" (a name Waddell at first despised so much that he tolerated its use only by his intimates).

Connie and Ban Johnson shared many of the same ideals. Both of them had finally got a belly full and had turned their backs on the gamblers who had corrupted whole ball clubs in the 1880s. (Connie's Buffalo club was once advised by the local paper to "fold up if it could not play a square game.") Connie and Ban also agreed in their distaste for players who were addicted to the bottle — the only difference was that Connie himself was a temperance man, while Ban became a notorious drinker. They were alike in their determination to put an end to the bullying of umpires and to rowdyism of all sorts. (Ban actually tried to put an end to all making of "concerted noises" by fans — but in that effort he struck out.)

Unfortunately, Connie wound up with several spasmodic drunks on his roster, including Rube Waddell, but he dealt with them as he dealt with all his players — gently, patiently, doing all his scolding in private, working them hard in their periods of sobriety, and forgiving them their trespasses. Connie believed in never finding fault with a ballplayer in front of his mates. He always let the man settle down after a bad mistake before calling him aside and trying to explain to him his error.

In Milwaukee, at the start, Connie still put on a uniform and occasionally "helped out" at first base or behind the plate. But he found that when he shared the locker room with his players he sometimes became embroiled in the name-calling and finger-pointing that often followed a loss. One day he grew so hot during an argument that he dared not speak lest he totally lose control in front of his players. After that, he took care to change his working clothes in private, and to conduct all discussions with players on a one-to-one basis.

Connie's worst problem at Milwaukee was trying to keep his gifted third baseman, Charlie Myers, in condition to play. To keep Charlie out of the taverns, Connie had to suspend and fine him periodically; he'd get a few weeks of top-notch play out of the infielder, then would have to suspend him again. But most of Connie's players were devoted and hard-working, many of them already of major-league ability even before Connie expertly nurtured their talents. In the outfield, he had a young man named Buck Weaver, formerly of Cleveland and Louisville in the National League. Many people were amazed to find Buck playing for Milwaukee and working so faithfully for Connie — for Buck was the man who had lost his temper a few seasons earlier over Connie's bat-tipping stunt and had turned Connie's hand into hamburger. Fortunately, Connie never carried grudges any longer than overnight and he seldom woke up mad at anyone.

Connie never even lost his temper at Rube Waddell, whom he soon managed to break to harness although half a dozen other men had failed. He first ran into Rube in 1899, when Rube — on his one-man strike against the Pittsburgh club, who at the time owned his contract — was pitching for the Columbus–Grand Rapids club. In that year he won twenty-eight games and accomplished two hundred strikeouts. The following season, Connie, seeking "just one more good pitcher" for his Milwaukee club, went looking for Rube and learned he was playing ball in Punxsutawney, Pennsylvania. So Connie took off for Punxsutawney and on the way stopped in Pittsburgh to get permission from

Barney Dreyfuss, the Pittsburgh owner, to deal with Rube. Then he pushed on and found the hotel where Rube was staying. He called him on the phone and made the fatal social blunder of addressing the man who answered as "Rube."

All Connie got in reply was a snarling "Who the hell are you?" When Connie tried to explain why he had come, he received a profane assurance that Rube liked it right where he was. Then the phone was slammed down and the call cut off. From that time forth, Connie always addressed Rube as "Eddie."

He first addressed him that way in a long, pleading letter outlining all the advantages (including a higher salary) of playing in Milwaukee. There was no response from Rube, but Connie kept sending telegrams or letters every day for two weeks. And finally Rube sent a brief reply: "Come and get me."

Connie took off at once, and arrived in Punxsutawney by train at eight o'clock in the morning. But before he could take Rube home he had to "ransom" him by paying about a dozen tabs that Rube had scattered about town — at the tailor's, at the haberdasher's, at the express office (where $7.50 was due on a dog somebody had sent Rube as a gift), and finally at the pawnshop where Rube, with $25.00 out of Connie's pocket, liberated his watch. Connie also had to finance Rube's breakfast, which consisted of more than Connie could eat in a day. They had just about cash enough left to get them to Milwaukee.

Working for Connie, Rube was a roaring success, both on the diamond and at the gate. He averaged five strikeouts a game and kept the bleachers packed full on the days he pitched. Connie used to help excite the crowd (and implant proper respect in the enemy) by taking Rube out to the outfield to warm him up. Every now and then, he would allow one of Rube's fastballs to go by and whack the board fence with a crack like a cannon shot. The bleacher bugs then would howl with happiness, convinced that Connie had been scared right out of the path of Rube's mighty pitch.

Connie exhibited great skill in handling his wayward Eddie. He discovered very early that Rube's two passions were fancy clothes (particularly red neckties, of which he owned a suitcase full) and fishing, so he saw to it that these passions were periodically gratified. And one day he had an inspiration that worked so well it lost him the Rube altogether.

Desperate for a winning pitcher, Connie decided one day, after Rube had won the first game of a doubleheader in seventeen innings, that he would have to use Rube in the second game, too. So he promised Rube several days at a nearby fishing lake if he would go out and pitch the second game. Rube did and won it 2 to 0, then took off on a dead run for the fishing spot. Before he ever came back, Connie received a wire from Barney Dreyfuss in Boston ordering him to turn Rube back to the Pittsburgh team. Rube's great performance had made headlines in eastern sports pages and Barney decided he needed a good pitcher, too.

So Rube returned to Pittsburgh — after an emissary from the Milwaukee club, at Connie's suggestion, had loaded him down with fishing tackle, loud neckties, two-tone shoes, and silk shirts. But Rube did not want to play for Pittsburgh and he spent a good part of his time riding on fire engines. He fled to Los Angeles, where he consistently mowed down batters, often four and five in a row. By this time, the Western League had turned into the American League and Connie had been awarded control of the Philadelphia franchise, of which he owned 25 percent of the stock. Since there was no agreement between the National and American leagues to prevent him from doing so, Connie felt free to reach out to the Coast and bring Rube back to him again. He had to employ two Pinkerton detectives to keep Rube from getting right back off the train. But they brought Rube safely to Philadelphia and Connie kept him there, winning ball games, for six seasons. And he always called him "Eddie."

Connie in fact addressed most of his players by their given names, avoiding nicknames when he could. When talking about his players to other people he often used the term *Mister;* he might explain where he planned to play "Mr. Miller"—who was merely Bing Miller to everyone else—or he would perhaps talk about his hopes for "Mr. Cobb." But names of complex derivation sometimes proved too much for Connie. He never was able to come any closer to pronouncing Lou Boudreau's name than "Mr. Boordee."

Connie had to struggle hard in Philadelphia. With money from Ben Shibe—partner in a sporting-goods business with Al Reach, the famous member of the "old" Philadelphia Athletics of "amateur" days— Connie was able to get a ball park next door to a brewery and to lure a number of National League stars his way. He also used Charles Comiskey's trick of giving his club a name that still lived in baseball fame around Philadelphia—the Athletics. But his operation was so meagerly financed that it had trouble staying afloat and John McGraw, owner at that time of the Baltimore franchise in the new league, allowed that Philadelphia was a "white elephant" to the league operation. The Athletics flaunted white elephants on their pennants and uniforms for many years thereafter.

Eventually Connie began to win championships with clubs that were often led by young pitchers he had discovered and trained himself—men like Eddie Plank, Jack Coombs, Chief Bender (always "Albert" to Connie), Joe Bush, Bob Shawkey, Lefty Grove, George Earnshaw, and Herb Pennock. He raised up great catchers, too, including Wally Schang and Mickey Cochrane. Connie also traded players craftily and seemed to have an instinct not only for spotting baseball talent but for pinpointing the moment when talent began to fade. He earned a reputation as a clever man by unloading players who were past their prime at just the right time. But he was also able to rescue veterans other clubs had given up on and to squeeze a few winning seasons out of them. Even Waite Hoyt, the great New York "schoolboy" who had once starred for the Yankees — and who had almost given up on himself when he was traded by the Yanks to Detroit — became a winner again when Connie signed him for the Athletics.

Having seen his own small bankroll evaporate when the Players' League expired, Connie kept close watch on his dollar bills. While he offered what looked like fat salaries to men who had grown restless under the National League $2400 salary limitation, he never actually spoiled any of his stars by overloading their pay envelopes. Still, like John McGraw, he nursed a streak of sentiment toward heroes of another day. When the rest of the league turned its back on two of its greatest names, Ty Cobb and Tris Speaker (after both of them were reported to have discussed betting with other players on games in which they were involved), Connie welcomed them to his roster.

Early in his managing career, as has been noted, Connie had made a practice of changing his clothes in a cell of his own. Finally, when the club was all his, he began to appear on the bench in his street clothes, complete with hard collar and hard hat (straw in the summer, a derby in the cooler seasons). From his position there, he would direct the club by waving his scorecard — placing the outfielders, as he once explained (with no undue modesty), "where the fly balls would drop in their hands."

Connie was eighty-eight before he took himself off the bench. He had won nine American League pennants, three of them in a row, and five world championships. In 1948, when he was nearing retirement, Connie was given a special reception at an old-timers' game. When his name was called in introduction over the PA, he hopped out of the

CULVER PICTURES

Connie Mack (at right) and John McGraw at the 1911 World Series

dugout with a good deal more alacrity than some of the veterans who were forty years his junior had been able to manage. And he accepted his award in the familiar squeaky but firm and vibrant voice that had bedeviled batters for sixty-five years.

Even after he had "retired," Connie Mack remained close to the club and sized up its prospects with a calculating eye. Now that he was free of office burdens, he enjoyed writing long letters in a legible and firm longhand script — letters recalling some of the great games he had been involved in and wisely predicting that this player or that would be really great "in days to come."

LOUIS SOCKALEXIS

The First Cleveland Indian

When the Cleveland Spiders changed their names to the Cleveland Indians, they did so in honor of Louis Sockalexis, who was the first full-blooded Indian to play major-league baseball. Sockalexis, a Penobscot from Old Town, Maine, was not by any means the first Indian to play baseball. Alexander Cartwright, on his journey to California, had taught the elements of the game to Indians on the plains. In Saint Louis, in the 1860s, a full-blooded Indian named Tom Oran was third baseman and catcher for the Empire club, one of the fastest "amateur" clubs in town. But before Sockalexis, none had made it to the real majors.

Sockalexis was no untutored son of the wild. He was gentle, good-natured, well spoken, and well mannered. His ways were outgoing, his smile quick, and he talked like a Yankee farmer. If he were playing today he might have become a movie or television star, for he was tall, broad-shouldered, generously muscled, with luxuriant black hair and the straight-cut features often considered the ideal of masculine beauty.

COURTESY OF THE COLLEGE OF THE HOLY CROSS

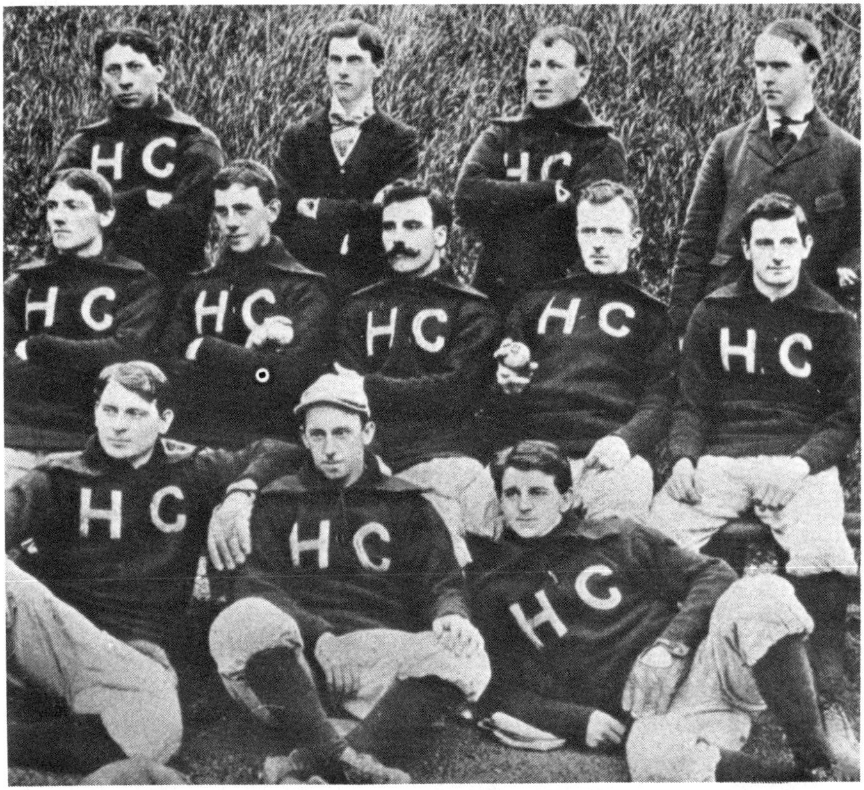

Louis Sockalexis (top row, far left) and the Holy Cross ball team of 1896

As an athlete, young Sockalexis could have excelled in any sport ever invented. He was big enough and tough enough for football and he could run a hundred yards, with his baseball shoes on, in ten seconds. But baseball, in the 1890s, was what every boy most wanted to play. Sockalexis learned the game on the sandlots around Old Town and first played it in an organized way in the Knox County League. There he was observed by Gilbert Patten, author of books about a fictional baseball player at Yale named Frank Merriwell who could work miracles, such as curving a baseball in two different directions on the same pitch. Sockalexis, of course, could not throw such a pitch, but if any real player had been able to throw a double curve, Sockalexis would have hit it: he could apparently — as they used to say before games were played under lights — "hit in the middle of the night." Patten was astonished at the Indian's abilities and talked him into applying for entrance at the College of the Holy Cross, where there was a special class for gifted athletes who might need a little help with their homework.

Sockalexis was long praised at Holy Cross and is still memorialized there, just as he is in Cleveland, where the American League club revived the name *Indians* long after the team had dropped out of the National League. Sockalexis became famous at college in his first year — for his hitting, for his arm, and for his speed on the bases. When the college team went on tour, Sockalexis would give throwing exhibitions before the games. From deep center field he would fire the ball in on a line to the catcher, right through the strike zone. His batting average in his first year at Holy Cross was .444!

There were stories circulating at the time alleging that Sockalexis was expelled from Holy Cross for drinking to excess, but it does not seem very likely that the college would have let go of its prize player for such a petty reason — drinking was the hobby of many a college boy bent on proving his masculinity in that day. Whatever the reason, Sockalexis showed up in the spring of 1896, after completing a season at Holy Cross, as a member of the ball team from the University of Notre Dame. A preseason game was arranged with the New York Giants, to give the famous Indian a chance to face the fastest pitcher in the league — Amos Rusie, the Indiana Thunderbolt, who, it was said, threw a curveball that was twice as fast as the fastball most other pitchers delivered.

The meeting between the two great players was trumpeted in the New York papers until the game drew as much attention as the World

Series. When Sockalexis appeared on the field, the Polo Grounds resounded with imitation war whoops, a greeting that thereafter became standard wherever Sockalexis appeared. In his first turn at bat, the young Indian stood up to the great Rusie without a show of fear. Relaxed and self-assured, he looked over both the steaming fastball and the whip-snapping curve. Then, with a swift, level swing, he drove the next curve far out toward the distant clubhouse. Before the scrambling Giants could make a play on him, the lithe young player had sped all the way around the bases for an inside-the-park home run.

That was but the first of many triumphs for Sockalexis. Monte Ward, former manager of the Giants, was in the stands that day and he immediately wrote to manager Pat Tebeau of Cleveland about the wonders he had seen. Because one of Tebeau's outfielders, Jess Burkett, often helped out as coach at Holy Cross, Pat already had some knowledge of the Indian. He invited him to Cleveland and signed him to a contract.

Sockalexis showed up to play for the Cleveland club in the spring of 1897 in perfect condition. If he had ever been guilty of "excessive drinking," there was no sign of it then in his clear, bright eyes, nor in his trim, hard-muscled body. Soft-spoken and smiling as always, Sockalexis — called "Sox" by his mates — was soon the most popular player in the locker room, despite the old-time tradition of looking upon every young recruit (especially a college boy) with scorn and hazing him without letup.

In his first practice game, Sox drove two pitches nearly to the fence and threw out two runners at the plate from deep right field. Pat Tebeau, who had signed Sox for $1500, promptly raised his salary to $2400. When the season opened, Pat may have regretted his impulsiveness for a moment, because Sox in the opening game seemed unable to get his bat on the ball. But next day was different. Facing "Still Bill"

Hill, Louisville's outsize rookie pitcher (who was on his way to striking out 104 batters that season), Sockalexis returned to college form and banged out two long hits. From that time until midseason, Sox hardly played a game without an extra-base blow.

The joy with which the victory-hungry Cleveland fans (whose team had not won a pennant since entering the league) greeted their adopted Indian was wilder than any demonstration that had ever greeted Sockalexis before. The home park was crowded even for the least important games and Tebeau reckoned Sox's value at the gate as higher than any star the club had ever owned. Not even the great Cy Young, nor the mighty Jess Burkett, nor the deer-footed Bobby Wallace, drew the crowds or attracted the attention Sox was getting.

The trouble was that Sox began to draw too much attention. Doors opened wherever he walked and men meeting him on the street vied with one another to invite him to share a drink at their expense. It was not in Sockalexis's nature to refuse a friendly invitation, and for a time his off-diamond doings seemed to have no effect upon his play.

Instead of tapering off, excitement seemed to intensify with every game Sox played. "Tebeau's Injun" became the most famous man throughout the National League circuit. He became the very symbol of the Cleveland ball club, with cartoons and war whoops greeting him in every city. The long-legged and angular athletes known as the Spiders had long ago left the Cleveland club, so the team became the Indians now and the players accepted their redskin status with unrestrained glee. Tomahawks and feather headdresses decorated programs; cartoonists pictured Sockalexis as a bigger-than-life painted figure in a warbonnet with a baseball bat for a war club. One nameless genius even wrote a poem — a chant — entitled "Sockalexis, Chief of Sock-em."

By July, Sockalexis was batting well over .400 and seemed sure to lift his average into incredible numbers. But more and more he was showing the effects of nights spent in reckless celebration. Pat Tebeau scolded him, benched him, fined him, even threatened him with dismissal, unless Sox learned to shun liquor — but to no avail. Finally, Pat promised Sox a salary of $6,000 — plus one of $10,000 the following season — if only he would pledge himself to sobriety. This was as good a deal as the greatest stars in the game were receiving, even with under-the-table bonuses.

Sox pledged, then promptly forgot the pledge. On the night before the Fourth of July, traditionally a night for painting the town in rainbow colors and setting off cannon-crackers, Sockalexis, in a moment of high exhilaration, leaped out of a two-story window and broke his foot on the sidewalk below. Sox hardly winced at the injury though. He bandaged the foot himself and hobbled down to join the team for its trip to Pittsburgh.

Pat Tebeau arrived the next day in Pittsburgh, hurried out to the ball park, and found the unhappy Indian sitting in the omnibus with his foot swollen to the size of a watermelon. Pat immediately ordered him back to the hotel in Cleveland and had the doctor encase his foot in a cast, with orders that Sockalexis should not so much as turn over in bed.

Sockalexis bore all this attention in silence. And when the doctor was gone he climbed out of bed and made his way to a saloon half a block away to solace himself with whiskey. As far as Tebeau was concerned, that was the end: he bought his pet player a ticket back to Old Town and bade him good-bye.

At home, Sockalexis came to his senses and began to mourn the triumphs he had known. He vowed once more never to raise liquor to his lips and he sent word of this vow to Tebeau, apologizing for his sixteen outfield errors and his failing batting average. All winter he sent declarations of penitence to Tebeau, pleading for one more chance to demonstrate the strength of his new conviction. Finally Tebeau gave in, and Sockalexis reported to Cleveland again in the spring.

But Sockalexis's abstinence lasted no longer than the crocuses that bloomed in the spring. Between drinking bouts, he managed to appear in just twenty-one games and made but fifteen base hits — only two for extra bases. A good part of the time he was in no shape to take his place on the diamond at all. Unable to move him by either threats or promises, Tebeau shipped him off to the bush leagues; from there, sad and lonely, Sockalexis quickly made his way back to Maine.

The next season, Lave Cross took over as Cleveland's manager and apparently persuaded himself that with a gentle approach he might succeed with the great Indian ballplayer, since Patsy Tebeau's tough techniques had failed. So Cross sent for Sockalexis and put him back in right field. Sockalexis, upon receipt of his first paycheck, began to drink again and was promptly set on the bench. He stayed dry for days and begged to be forgiven. Lave forgave him and put him back in the line-up, but Sockalexis quickly forgot his pledge. He was benched again, took the pledge again, and was forgiven again. This routine was repeated two or three times before Lave Cross admitted to himself that Sockalexis was a lost cause and told Sox he was through. But a few nights later, instead of making the rounds of taverns, Sockalexis showed up at Lave Cross's hotel room and tearfully begged for one last chance. Now, at last, he had surely, *surely* learned his lesson. He had not touched whiskey for days and never would again.

Lave Cross gave in once again and restored Sockalexis to the lineup for a final trial. The Cleveland club was playing Saint Louis and their pitcher was Jack Powell, who had been Sox's teammate the year before. Jack greeted his former pal by throwing the baseball right at Sox's head. Sockalexis, who was reputed never to have lost his temper, flew into a rage at this treachery. He pounded the plate in a fury and drove the

COURTESY OF THE CLEVELAND INDIANS

In the last years of his career, Sox played for the Castine, Maine, team

next pitch on a screaming line to left center for two bases. Then he hit safely his next four times at bat. Teammates and fans yelled in delirious admiration and Sockalexis decided the world was his again.

That night Sockalexis hastened back to the bottle to celebrate his return to glory. By the time he had come back close enough to earth to take note of what others were up to, he found that the ball club had left town without him. So he went to the theater with some friends and loudly expressed his dismay and anger during the performance. This landed poor Sockalexis in jail and his major-league career was finally over.

Sockalexis then signed up with some minor-league clubs, drifting lower and lower each time. He played with Hartford, then with Lowell, Massachusetts, and finally settled for bread-and-beans jobs with semi-pro clubs throughout New England. Ultimately, he became a tramp, and old men used to recall, a few decades ago, how they had occasionally met the great Sockalexis huddled over a tiny fire in a hobo jungle: frowsy, tattered, bloated in the face, just a caricature of the handsome, clean-limbed Indian who was going to set the world on fire — the man who could throw a baseball farther and straighter than any man ever had before and who could hit a pitched ball with power no white player ever possessed. Louis Sockalexis ended his days back in Old Town, Maine, running a ferry. He died of heart failure when he was only forty-two years old.

JOE WILLIAMS

The Texas Cyclone

Years ago, one of the finest pitchers in the country — one who could find a good payday in any of a hundred cities where there were promoters to stage exhibition baseball games — was a man who had been kept out of the major leagues because, as he put it, his "hair was too curly." The real reason Joe Williams was not allowed to pitch big-league ball, of course, was that he was black. When he was active, in the early 1900s, there was not even a glimmer of hope that the lily-white majors would admit black ballplayers.

But there was hardly a white pitcher in the whole nation who could fire the ball as steadily, as fast, and as accurately as lean Joe Williams could. He was ready to prove this fact in exhibition games on any Sunday when he was not busy pitching ball games in the Negro National League. Again and again he sent major-league hitters home declaring they had never in their lives seen the ball thrown so fast as Joe Williams threw it. For Joe was "Cyclone Joe" in his glory days — the swiftest pitcher throughout the Negro leagues. Whether he was as fast or faster than Satchel Paige (who's discussed later on), no one ever can say for sure. But he was fast enough to strike out almost all the white hitters who faced him.

In 1912 (when Satchel Paige was just six years old), Joe Williams pitched his first game against a major-league club — beating the New York Giants, National League pennant winners, by a score of 6 to 0 on a cramped Harlem field. Cyclone Joe retired from baseball twenty years later, not much richer than when he started, and went to tending bar in a Harlem saloon.

When he was at his best, Joe was a solidly built man with powerful shoulders and a lean, hard body. He stood six-foot-five and weighed 210 pounds. But he was a skinny kid in 1900 when he began to pitch for money — just fourteen years old and a member of the Black Broncos, of San Antonio, Texas, where he was born and raised. His most devoted fan then was his mother, who used to come to every Bronco game, traveling sometimes thirty miles to sit on a front-row bench and cry out to the opposing club: "You can't beat my Joe!"

His mother was right, for there were very few ballplayers in that area who could even raise a foul off young Joe's smoking fastball. Before he turned fifteen Joe was invited to travel to Cuba with a black all-star team to play on the island for real money. Every winter, for the rest of his career, Joe played baseball in Cuba.

After he returned from that first trip to the Caribbean, Joe's family moved to Chicago, and he never played ball in Texas again. He played semipro ball in Chicago for ten years, sometimes pitching for clubs on which he was the only black player. He earned enough to get by until winter began and he could get back to Cuba, where black men could earn as much as whites on the baseball diamond.

Joe was twenty-six years old, with a lot of baseball behind him, when he joined the Lincoln Giants, as manager and pitcher. With this club he became famous throughout the whole land.

Joe's first triumph with the Lincoln Giants came in his first assignment, a 6-to-0 victory over a white semipro club called the New York Ironsides. It was soon after that that he met the Giants and shut them out. The next year, before taking off for Cuba, Joe toured the Pacific Coast League and beat every club he faced except Portland. He was pitching on that tour for the Leland Giants, owned by the great black organizer Rube Foster, and he won nine games for Rube out of eleven he pitched.

Joe won two of those games in a single day; after he had taken the first game of a doubleheader against Seattle, 2 to 1, the pitcher for the Leland Giants in the second game could not get any of the first three batters out. Rube Foster, in desperation, hustled to the locker room to bring Joe back.

"I'll give you fifty bucks if you get me out of this crack!" he told Joe.

Joe studied the matter for a few seconds, then asked: "Fifty more if I win?"

"Sure thing!" said Rube.

So Joe went back to warm up again. And when the fans saw who was getting ready to pitch, they began to fling money at his feet, all the while yelling in delight. Silver dollars and half-dollars came plunking onto the turf. Joe quietly gathered them all up and tucked them away before going to the mound. He gave Seattle only one hit and beat them 1 to 0.

But the victory he most liked to recall was not that one, nor even the times he beat those fine pitchers Rube Marquard and Grover Cleveland Alexander. His fondest memory was his no-hit shutout against his bitterest rival — "Cannonball" Dick Redding, who dared to rate himself the best black pitcher of the day. Dick, whose fastball almost matched Joe's, did indeed pitch great baseball for the Brooklyn Royal Giants on the day he hurled against Joe Williams. But Joe was even greater: he faced just twenty-nine batters in nine innings, walked but one — and knocked in the winning run, the only run, with a hit of his own.

Next to that, perhaps Joe treasured most the recollection of the day the Lincoln Giants met the pennant-winning Philadelphia Phillies and Joe beat them 1 to 0, allowing the Phillies only four hits and striking out ten batters.

There were great men playing for the Phillies that day in 1915, including Dave Bancroft, who was called Beauty because he habitually called out "Beauty!" when the pitcher sent a strike past him; Joe Judge, then a hard-hitting rookie borrowed from Washington just for this game; Gavvy Cravath, who led his league in home runs; and George Chalmers, who had posted an earned run average of 2.48.

Playing on Joe's side was his favorite catcher and his best friend in baseball, Wabishaw S. "Doc" Wiley, a dental student who eventually set up practice in New Jersey. Frank Forbes, who became a famous prizefight judge, played shortstop that day for the Lincoln Giants.

The teams met at Olympic Field (at 136th Street and Fifth Avenue), a somewhat undersized park where the Lincoln Giants played their home games (the team had originated in Lincoln, Nebraska — hence the name). Harlem was not yet a black ghetto in 1915, and there were many spectators both black and white in the crowded stands who were cheering for a boy who had grown up in Harlem — George Chalmers, the Phillies' pitcher. Most of the black spectators, however — and many of the white — were rooting for Joe Williams and his teammates. There were no hard feelings and no racial nicknames being shouted.

The local fans were delighted to have the big-leaguers come play in this Harlem backyard and they were so worked up at the spectacle, Joe said afterward, "they didn't have no time to talk. Just yell."

Joe was a striking man in his youth, with skin the color of bronze, the face of a warrior chief, and shoulders heavy with muscle. He always worked calmly on the mound and often smiled when he was in trouble, as if he were amused at the problem that faced him and was going to enjoy untangling it. His problems that day against the Phillies were few; his famous control seldom wavered, his fastball whistled, and the curve broke sharply down to the batters' knees.

Only in the fourth inning did Cyclone Joe seem to falter a little. He walked the first two batters. The yelling from the crowd grew louder. Joe's infield beseeched him to start pouring in the strikes. Joe looked around and smiled his gentle smile, shook his head as if surprised that anyone could doubt him, then fired a fastball to Joe Judge. Joe swung mightily, but he just topped the ball and it dribbled into the infield. Before anyone could capture the lazily rolling ball, Joe Judge had made it to first. Now the bases were full and Cyclone Joe Williams was *really* in trouble. But he didn't think so: he stepped back, checked over the men on bases, hunched his mighty shoulders, and began to fire the ball with his full strength.

Joe struck out the next two batters. The third man barely topped Joe's fiery pitch and rolled the ball back to the pitcher's mound. Joe threw him out.

By the eighth inning no one on either team had scored and the crowd of 9000 had begun to yell with every pitch. In the bottom half of the inning, Frank Forbes, batting eighth, worked Chalmers for a base on balls. Joe Williams, who loved his base hits, promptly moved Forbes ahead with a single. With men on first and second, the leadoff man laid down a sacrifice bunt that put runners on second and third. After that the third baseman, a rugged fellow named Bragg, lined a long single to center, scoring Frank Forbes.

That was the only run scored in the ball game. In the ninth inning, Joe again let his control slip a little and put three men on base. But then he hunched his mighty shoulders again, smiled to himself, shook his head once or twice — and struck out the next three batters on nine consecutive pitches! The entire crowd exploded with admiration.

Not long after that victory, the major leagues adopted a rule that forbade post-season games in which major-league teams appeared as units. It just would not do to have black teams destroying league "champions" in this manner.

Joe Williams then had another seventeen years of baseball ahead of him, in which he would travel around the whole country, beating clubs of every quality, black and white. He later joined the Brooklyn Royal Giants, where his rival Dick Redding had long been a leader, and he played as well for the Leland Giants and for several all-star clubs (on which he was usually the greatest star). He often expressed mild regret that he had learned baseball under rules that required the pitcher to keep both feet in contact with the rubber before delivering a pitch. If he had been able to "rear back" in the style of Dazzy Vance, Bob Feller, and Dizzy Dean, thus adding a long stride to his delivery, he might have put another few pounds of power into his speed and struck out half the men who faced him.

Joe occasionally resorted to a knuckleball to throw the batters off balance, but he had no use for the spitter. His delivery was straight overhand, so that he had plenty of "air" in which to add snap to his curve. This pitch, delivered with the same motion as his mighty fastball, would break and dive almost straight down, like a speeding bird shot dead in midflight. Joe's control was so sharp that he could keep his pitches down near the batters' knees inning after inning. And he was ready to pitch every day, if he was called on, or even twice a day if there was a few extra dollars in it. It was the game itself that he really loved, however — far more than what cash it brought him. Joe's earnings never equaled those of Satchel Paige or some of the showier performers, but he made a good living and lasted in the game far longer than most men did.

After a spell with the Brooklyn Royal Giants (who were named after the Royal Café), Joe Williams signed on with the Homestead Grays of Pittsburgh to manage and pitch, as he had with the Lincoln Giants. He stayed with this club until 1932, when he was forty-six, and then he had to admit he could no longer take his turn on the mound. The next year, Joe was called on to pitch in a charity benefit game against the New York Police Department team; he worked two innings and gave up neither a hit nor a run. After that, Cyclone Joe never played baseball again.

Behind his bar in Harlem, where he grew gray (but never soft and fat), Joe used to love to recall his best days on the diamond, counting over not only his strikeouts but his hits, and describing the meetings he had with the great pitchers of his day.

"Lefty Gomez was the only big-league pitcher ever beat me twice," he would say. "Once in Charles Town [Charleston], West Virginia, and once in Jamestown, New York. A long time ago." Joe had lost once to Rube Marquard, then beat the Rube the next time they met. He also split decisions with the mighty Grover Cleveland Alexander, when "Old Pete" had just finished a season in which he won thirty-one games.

Joe Williams took pride in the fact that, although he pitched in an era when pitchers used to doctor the ball in a dozen ways to make it move toward the plate in an erratic manner, he stuck to his fastball and curve — "except when the other guy started using tricks."

"Did I use the emery ball" — Joe said with a grin one day — "I'd have won every game."

HAROLD (HAL) CHASE

Prince of First Basemen

Harold "Hal" Chase, the greatest first baseman who ever played and the man who really perfected the dash in to the plate to grab sacrifice bunts, has no spot in baseball's Hall of Fame and never will — for he was almost certainly guilty of throwing ball games or arranging to have them thrown so that he and his associates might win bets. He lost his job on the Cincinnati Reds for "indifferent playing," which meant he had been trying not to win. He was called up before the president of the National League on a charge of deliberately losing ball games. His manager, pitcher Christy Mathewson, had noticed that Hal would sometimes mess up one of the simplest plays in the game — a toss to the pitcher covering first after the first baseman had fielded the ball. Again and again Hal, the "perfect" fielder, would flip the ball just wide enough of the bag that the pitcher was pulled off the base and the runner was safe. After Mathewson had talked over this situation with the club owner, Hal Chase was released and a hearing was held by John Heydler, league president.

NATIONAL BASEBALL HALL OF FAME

Hal Chase

By the time of the hearing, held in midwinter, Mathewson had joined the army and gone to France. The other witnesses all concentrated on one contest, a game in which Hal Chase hit a home run that won the game; so it hardly seemed likely he could have been betting against his own club. The charges therefore were dismissed and Hal's name was "cleared." But he was never cleared in the eyes of some of the officials, and after John McGraw had taken on Chase to play first base for the New York Giants, Heydler continued his investigation. He finally came up with some canceled checks given to a Boston bookmaker that indicated Chase had indeed bet against his own team at times. He was promptly fired by McGraw and never played big-league ball again. McGraw even forbade his players to be seen in conversation with Chase.

You might imagine that Chase was a sort of fiend in human form — but Hal was just the opposite. A handsome, well-built young man with bright red hair and a lively, good-humored countenance, he was friendly with everyone, although he had no close friends at all. Hal, full of funny stories, was an excellent mimic; he was generous — quick to lend a dollar or buy a round of drinks — and skilled at every indoor or outdoor sport ever invented. He was a sharpster with a billiard cue, a dead shot with a rifle, a competent boxer, a skilled poker player, and an adept horseman. His only ambition in life seemed to be to grab a fast dollar as often as he could and to have fun every minute.

Hal, born in Los Gatos, in the California desert, started out by trying to become a civil engineer. He was a great baseball player in high school and an all-around success on the athletic fields at Santa Clara College, however, so he never became an engineer.

When he was twenty years old, after winning headlines as a star on the college nine, Hal took a job playing "independent" (semipro) ball in Canada. While there he played every infield position, as well as catcher, and his accomplishments won him a salaried job with the Los Angeles club of the Pacific Coast League. He played so spectacularly, in his 173 games, that he was drafted by the New York American League club — sarcastically known as the "Burglars" and the "Porch Climbers," because they had sneaked into the upper reaches of Manhattan when the National League was trying to close them out. (The team's official name was "Highlanders.")

In New York, Hal found himself among some hard-boiled lads who were not inclined to eye a college boy with favor. And Hal made no secret of the fact that he considered himself a good deal smarter than his teammates. So the fielders used to take care to aim their throws to first into the dirt, where Hal would have to dig them out. Or they would send them high above his head where he would have to leap for them. But Hal caught them all, and grinned as he did so. There was just no such thing as a throw within human reach that he could not field. The spectators were enraptured by such play and sportswriters dubbed Chase "Prince Hal" in honor of his superiority. Even his teammates then began to observe that Hal was the best in the business.

Hal was also one of the best with a bat. His first manager in New York, Clark Griffith, said he never knew Hal to miss laying down a perfect bunt on a squeeze play. He was unmatched, too, at hitting behind a moving runner on a hit-and-run play. Prince Hal could also rattle hits off the board fence when he found pitches that he favored.

In his fifth year with New York, however, Hal grew impatient with the scolding of his new manager, Norman Elberfeld, known as "the Tabasco Kid" because of the temper of his tongue. Elberfeld, who always found fault with everyone, found constant fault with happy-go-lucky Chase (who had once plunged the whole clubhouse into gloom by persuading the players all to bet on a horse named Clark Griffith, who ran out of the money). Hal's habits of coming and going as he pleased, dressing carelessly and incompletely, picking up bets in the clubhouse, organizing high-stakes card games, and taking off on Sunday (when there was no league ball) to pick up extra dollars playing with a sandlot nine were not forgiven by the Tabasco Kid just because Hal played like a magician. Hal was subjected almost daily to Elberfeld's summations reviewing his sins — until finally Hal, who habitually did as he damn well pleased, walked off the club and took a job with an "outlaw" team in Stockton, California.

Behavior of that sort was supposed to mean a five-year suspension. But the New York fans set up such a clamor that Hal was forgiven and returned to the roster in 1909, whereas Elberfeld was packed off to find some other team to yell at. In 1910, the New York management had so lost good sense that it made Hal himself manager. That ignoble experiment lasted two seasons; then Hal was reduced to the ranks and Frank Chance became manager.

Chance was deaf in one ear, and when Hal learned this he amused himself by sitting on Chance's deaf side and imitating his instructions, even mimicking his expressions, to the delight of some of the other players. One player grew tired of this act and reported it to Chance, who took Hal's job away from him then swapped him off to the Chicago White Sox.

When the Federal League was organized — providing a third "major" league, and a place where salaries were going to be higher and tickets would cost but twenty-five cents — Hal looked over his contract with Chicago. It provided, he observed, that the club could let him go on ten days' notice. On the reasonable assumption that turnabout was fair play, Hal gave ten days' notice of his departure and signed with the Federal League club in Buffalo. Charles Comiskey took Hal to court over the move and the court ruled in Hal's favor — a decision that might then and there have wrecked the reserve clause, had anyone decided to force the issue. But the Federal League collapsed after one season and Hal wound up with the Cincinnati club of the National League, where Christy Mathewson began to take note of his suspicious behavior.

After Heydler had barred Hal Chase from organized baseball, Hal spent his days largely in the Far West and the Southwest, where outlaw baseball clubs flourished in half a hundred towns and where he could always find room on a roster. But he could never match the money he was making in Cincinnati when he drew a salary of almost $9000 — considered a juicy take in that day. So Hal consoled himself more and

A quick throw from first

more with drinking. He had broken up with his wife after four years of marriage and never really had a home again. Sometimes he would spend all night in a tavern. Hal's skills with bat, ball, and billiard cue were slow to leave him, so he never lacked funds for another drink. But often, like so many steady drinkers, he forgot to eat; he came down at last with a strange vitamin-deficiency disease called beriberi, common among the wretched poor of India. This ailment was what finally killed him — but he had lived sixty-four years before that always doing what he felt like doing at the moment. Had he been less addicted to picking up a dishonest dollar, Prince Hal's accomplishments on the diamond would have earned him lasting glory (or he might have made a name as a boxer or wrestler).

Hal played the game of baseball in his own way. He was left-handed, yet preferred to bat right-handed — for no reason that anyone could understand. He did all his sliding to base headfirst, yet he stole 330 bases while he was playing in the major leagues. His reflexes were so incredibly fast that on a squeeze play he sometimes would catch a bunt before it hit the ground, then tag the approaching runner out to complete an unassisted double play. Many times, when he charged in to field a sacrifice bunt, Hal would slap a tag on the batter, then rifle the ball to a baseman to nail the lead runner, too.

Hal committed many errors, though — he usually led the league in errors at his position. But these were not often — or not always — the result of poor play or deliberate attempts to miss. He would try for hard ground balls and for wild throws that ordinary first basemen would not go near. And often he was given an error because his lightning throw reached a base before the baseman had got there and prepared to receive it.

When Hal was thirty-three, in 1916, he led the National League in batting average and in total hits. In his one season in the Federal League he was the league leader in home runs, with seventeen. Because he played baseball or other games the year round, he was always in excellent condition to play — and if Hal Chase had played the game straight, he might have put twenty years or more in the major leagues, perhaps setting marks no one could have surpassed.

JAY HANNA DEAN

The Original "Dizzy"

There were a number of baseball players in the past generation who tried to name themselves — or were named by sportswriters — "Dizzy" or "Daffy." But there was only one Dizzy Dean and there will never be another. Except for a minor injury that forced him to alter his pitching motion, Dizzy might have turned into the greatest pitcher ever. (Or at least the second greatest — Dizzy, who loved to brag about his ability, still would have allowed that his brother Paul, or Satchel Paige, was even better.)

Dizzy gave himself two different names, claimed three different birthplaces, and invented several different life stories. Like so many boys who came up out of deep poverty, he felt an urge to build himself a more interesting personality by making up stories about his past. For a while he called himself "Jerome Herman Dean," and even Branch Rickey, the man he worked for, long called him "Jerome." He gave his birthplace sometimes as Holdenville, Oklahoma, sometimes as Bond, Mississippi; and sometimes he gave the correct answer: Lucas, Arkan-

NATIONAL BASEBALL HALL OF FAME

Dizzy Dean

sas. He took the name *Jerome Herman* to honor the memory of a boyhood friend who died, or at least that is how he explained it. One time he gave his middle name as *Hanner*—although actually his father had named him after Mark Hanna, the Republican boss who had helped make William McKinley President before young Jay was born. Dizzy also solemnly explained once that he had first turned to pitching at Oklahoma City Teachers' College—a school he never entered. (Perhaps if he had, he would have lost the rich vernacular that used to delight listeners after Dizzy turned to radio broadcasting.)

Dizzy received most of his schooling on the run; his father, an itinerant cotton picker, traveled from one job to the next, bringing along the small family he had been left with when Dizzy's mother died. Dizzy himself, from the time he was old enough to pick his weight in cotton, earned two dollars a day working at his father's side. Like Mickey Mantle's father, Dizzy's father had been a semipro baseball player himself, and he liked to see his boys playing the game. He kept them supplied with a baseball or two and enough makeshift equipment to enable them to play some sort of game among themselves when there was time to spare. Jay had two brothers: a younger one, Paul; and an older one, Elmer.

But where Jay really learned baseball was in the army, which he joined when he was sixteen. He was a big, husky boy and when he told the recruiting sergeant he was eighteen the sergeant believed him. Jay by this time had acquired two stepbrothers, both of whom were already in the army, and they had talked Jay into enlisting — not so he could learn baseball, but so he could eat better and keep regular hours.

Jay, however, found it difficult to adjust his nature to army discipline and was forever pulling KP because of some infraction. But when soldiers started playing baseball, life began to look brighter. Almost at once, Jay became the star pitcher for the Twelfth Field Artillery, stationed at Fort Sam Houston, in San Antonio, Texas, and began to earn himself a reputation in the area as a lad who threw the baseball hard. He had signed on for four years, but before his stretch was quite completed, he begged his father to buy his release, even though he had only three months to go before discharge. The elder Dean had run into a stretch of good earnings and was able to come up with the necessary $120 to set young Jay free.

Thereupon Jay took a job with the San Antonio Public Service Corporation as a meter reader. But he did not do any meter reading. The agreement was that he was to pitch for the company ball club to earn his fat salary of thirty dollars a week (the prospect of this job was undoubtedly what made him impatient to leave the army). Now eighteen years old, Jay had reached his full height and strength, and the fastball he fired now would make even a big-leaguer blink. Working in the industrial league in San Antonio, Jay began to be talked about. Eventually a railroad conductor passed the word to a big-league scout (who also worked for the railroad) that there was a young pitcher nearby who threw nothing but smoke. The scout was Don Curtis, a bird dog for the Saint Louis Cardinals. He took time off to watch Jay pitch in a few ball games; then he asked the boy to come talk to him about a contract. Within hours, Jay had signed to play the following spring with Houston in the Texas League — for $300 a month, which was, in 1930, a rich man's salary to young Dean.

Dean got his first chance to exhibit his extraordinary skills in an exhibition game between Houston and the Chicago White Sox. Dean struck out so many of the big-leaguers that the Cardinal bosses decided to move him no further down than Class A, with Saint Joseph of the Western League.

In Saint Joseph, Jay earned his nickname "Dizzy" and kept it the rest of his life. (His wife always called him "Jay," though, and his friends eventually took to calling him "Country.") Dizzy knew nothing about suitcases or about checking in and out of hotels. He moved to Saint Joseph with only the clothes he wore and at one time or another he checked into three different hotels, choosing whichever one happened to be handiest. When his shirt seemed too dirty to go another round, he bought a new shirt and tossed the old one in a bureau drawer. Hotel bills and clothing bills he charged to the ball club.

Dizzy was wild in the Western League — wild on the mound and wild off the diamond. He one time beat up a first baseman, once walked ten batters in a single game, and another time was arrested for driving sixty-five miles an hour right through the middle of town (but he made friends with the police chief). Dizzy started a triple play in one game; he also struck out a boatload of ballplayers and by the first week in August had a record of seventeen wins and eight losses. The Cardinal brass took special note of Dizzy now and decided that he was not working in fast enough company. They shifted him at once back to the club that had first checked him out — Houston in the Texas League, one notch below the majors.

On the very night he arrived in Houston, Dizzy took to the mound against San Antonio and won by a score of 12 to 1, striking out fourteen batters. He won his next five games in a row. Pitching against Beaumont, he struck out sixteen. It was no surprise to anyone therefore when, in September, the Saint Louis Cardinals sent for him to come join the big club in New York for a trial period. But Dizzy did not pitch in a Saint Louis uniform until the end of the month, after the Cardinals had already clinched the pennant. Then he was sent out to be "seasoned" by the murderous Pittsburgh Pirates, who carried such fearsome sluggers as Pie Traynor, Paul Waner and his brother Lloyd (known respectively as Big and Little Poison), as well as "Rowdy Dick" Bartell. But the great men all looked alike to Dean, who was surprised, after beating them 3 to 1, that they had actually got three hits off him.

Dizzy really should have joined the big team permanently the next season, 1931, for he was obviously a big-leaguer and, while Saint Louis was powerful without him, they'd have been more powerful still — and would have pulled more customers in — if they had taken him aboard. But Dizzy was denied promotion chiefly because he was too cocky. He addressed his betters by their first names and he kept charging expenses to the club without permission — and he bragged about how many games he was going to win for Saint Louis.

Although Dizzy was no drunkard, nor one to stay out late (one of his more heinous sins was buying ice-cream sodas for a bunch of high-school girls every day and charging them to the management), the Saint Louis brass felt they had to put him in his place. So they returned him to the Texas League, where Dizzy won 26 games while losing 10, struck out 303 batters, and posted an earned run average of 1.53. He also made a number of important base hits and once pitched all afternoon and won both games of a doubleheader. He also got married — to a girl he met in a department store.

Next season, the Cardinals simply could not keep Dizzy off the roster and he became one of the most spectacular members of the famous Gashouse Gang. At the start of the season, when he complained that he was not being worked often enough, there were whispers that he would be demoted once more until he learned to keep his mouth shut, but he promptly won a shutout against Chicago and the management decided it could stand a little fresh talk. They also thereafter worked him often enough so he had nothing to complain about. In August he pitched and won 3 games in five days. He won 18 games his first season. He had predicted in 1931, the year he was sent back to Texas, that he would win 30. In 1933 he made no predictions. But he won 20 games, struck out seventeen batters in one game, and stirred the management to wrath again by missing an exhibition game. ("I must have got on the wrong train," Dizzy explained.) He also persuaded the Cardinals to sign his brother Paul. ("Besides Paul," said Dizzy, "I'm just a 'sem-eye' pro.")

In 1934, Dizzy made another prediction. Paul, who had won 20 and lost 7 for Columbus of the American Association, was now on the Cardinal staff. Dizzy prophesied that "Me and Paul" would win 45 games between them in 1934. Dizzy was wrong about that: together the Dean brothers won 49. They also won the pennant for the Cards, although it had been virtually conceded to the New York Giants, who

Dizzy showing the form that earned him his fame

had it "won," with only a few weeks to go. And then Dizzy, almost by himself, destroyed the Detroit Tigers in the World Series.

Dizzy continued to upset the club and league authorities by his devotion to free speech and eccentric behavior. He and Paul (Paul always followed Dizzy's lead) stayed home from an exhibition game and then went on a two-man strike when they were respectively fined $100 and $50. When manager Frank Frisch suspended them and told them to take off their uniforms if they were not going to play, Dizzy and Paul not only removed their uniforms but tore them into rags. And, when newsreel photographers complained that they had missed the tearing-up ceremony, Dizzy and Paul, for the benefit of the press, tore up their road uniforms, too. This performance wound up with a hearing before Judge Landis (the baseball commissioner), a reinstatement, and the loss of seven days' pay. To celebrate his return to the lineup, Dizzy won his twenty-second game, a 5–0 shutout over the Giants.

To watch Dizzy and brother Paul work that year was like seeing the same pitcher twice. Both had a generous windup and stride, with a three-quarter overhand delivery that never seemed to tire them. Dizzy would also throw sidearm or straight overhand at times to confuse the opposition. Both men were strong and fast. Dizzy's "crooky," as he called his curve, may have been sharper than Paul's, but both could throw great helpings of smoke.

One of Paul's victories that season was a no-hitter against Brooklyn pitched immediately after Dizzy had won the first game of a double-header, 13 to 0, allowing but three feeble hits. "I wish Paul would have told me he was going to pitch a no-hitter," said Diz. "Then I'd of throwed one, too."

In the 1934 World Series against the Detroit Tigers, Dizzy was irrepressible (even though not quite unbeatable). He posed for a picture while twisting the tail of a toy tiger. He inserted himself into the Detroit batting practice. And he asked Hank Greenberg, Detroit's home-run hero, to let him heft his bat. He took Hank's war club in hand, weighed it judiciously, then handed it back. "Throw it away," he said. "I'm pitchin'."

In the fourth game of the series, for some incomprehensible reason, manager Frisch allowed Dizzy to talk him into putting Dizzy in as a pinch runner. Dizzy could never stand to be far from the action when a big prize was at stake. So Dizzy ran from first to second on a ground ball and broke up a double play by failing to slide. He took the short-stop's throw right on the head and dropped unconscious on the baseline. He was rushed to the hospital, but assured everyone when he came to that he was not going to be sidelined by any little "hit on the haid."

Nor was he. He did lose the fifth game (he had won the first) but he pitched well enough to win; Tommy Bridges of Detroit simply pitched better. Paul, who had won the second game, won the sixth game, and it was Dizzy's job to win the seventh. He did this in proper Dean style, scattering six hits, and starting a seven-run rally with a double. The Tigers did not score at all, and Dizzy, in the later innings, strutted and clowned on the pitching mound, contorting himself, making faces, and playing the part of a sandlot pitcher. Manager Frisch tried to straighten Dizzy out by threatening to take him out of the game if he did not behave with more dignity.

"Oh no you won't," said Dizzy. "You wouldn't dare do that with all them people listening on the radio."

And Frisch didn't dare.

Having won 30 games that season while losing only 7 (for a league-leading won-lost average of .811), having struck out 195 batters to lead the league in that department, and having led the league in shutouts as well, Dizzy Dean was obviously on the way to becoming the greatest pitcher in organized baseball — in his own lifetime at least. There was talk of his holding out for some fantastic salary like $20,000, and, indeed, he signed for 1935 at a salary of $19,500. He was earning more than that from vaudeville appearances and from endorsements of merchandise — odds and ends from toothpaste to kites.

In 1935, Dizzy knew some bad moments but he continued to win. He was felled by a batted ball to the shin in one game and in another he had a row with his teammates, whom he accused of failing to do their best when he was pitching. When the teammates called him dirty names, Dizzy offered to battle the entire crew. Ducky Medwick, the tough outfielder, accepted the invitation and charged up to meet Dizzy on the first-base line. The two were held apart and Ducky stamped angrily back to the bat rack and picked up a bat. All he probably intended to do was drive a pitch as far as he could make it travel, but Paul Dean misunderstood the move and leaped out to grab hold of Ducky.

"Don't hit him with no bat!" Paul wailed. "I don't care what you do with your fists, but don't hit him with no bat!" Then poor Paul, overcome with emotion, dropped to the bench and burst into tears.

The team soon became reconciled, and Dizzy kept on winning games. He sulked once at being made to sit on the bench during an exhibition game; soon afterward he begged Frank Frisch to let him pitch every third day, so the club could gain some ground in the pennant race. But Frisch said every fourth day was enough. Dizzy won 28 games, struck out 182, and pitched 324⅓ innings, to lead the club in all those departments. The Cardinals, however, just missed winning the pennant.

Dizzy threatened again to hold out for a really big salary (he hinted at $40,000 and a three-year contract), but he settled again for a more moderate figure in 1936 and predicted firmly that the Cards would win the pennant. But 1936 was a hard-luck year for the whole club. While Dizzy kept winning ball games, Paul developed a sore arm and the other pitchers wobbled. So Dizzy, in addition to starting regularly, went to the bullpen every day too; he acted as relief pitcher in 17 games during the season and saved 11 of them. In all, he struck out 195 batters and won 24 games. But there were rough moments: Dizzy on one occasion took a batted ball in the head that knocked him unconscious. He also got into a fistfight with ex-teammate Tex Carleton and came out with a cut over one eye. And at the end of the season he had to admit he was tired and that his fastball had lost some of its zip. No wonder: he had won 82 games in three seasons and had pitched 951 innings.

But the next season Dizzy was his old self in every way—cocky, smart, eager to work, and out to have fun both on and off the diamond. He opened the season by pitching twenty scoreless innings in a row. And when the team went to Boston, he promised to strike out outfielder Vince DiMaggio, Joe's brother, four times in one game. He struck out poor Vince (who was the league-leader in striking out) three times. In his fourth time at bat, Dizzy got two strikes on Vince and then Vince hit an easy pop foul behind the plate. Catcher Bruce Ogrowdowski camped under it and got set to tuck it away. Dizzy was dismayed.

"Drop it!" he screamed. "Drop it!" So Bruce dutifully let it drop. Then Dizzy, grinning happily, returned to the mound and wheeled over a fastball to make it strikeout number four by Vince.

In mid-May, however, trouble began to appear. In a game with the Giants, Dizzy was penalized for failing to come to a complete stop in his pitching motion before delivering the ball to the plate. Dizzy raged at that and grew even more enraged when Jim Ripple of the Giants accused him of trying to hit him with a pitch; Ripple then dragged a bunt toward first to draw Dizzy into a collision. Dizzy took on the challenge, ran to field the ball, dumped Ripple on the baseline, and started a riot so fierce that the police had to pull the teams apart.

In his next start, Dizzy, who had been brooding over the balk called against him in the game with the Giants, decided to demonstrate how ridiculous the rule was. He paused so long after each stretch that the umpire first accused him of delaying the game and finally called a ball as a penalty after an especially long delay. Furious, Dizzy sat right down on the mound and refused to proceed. The umpire threatened to kick him out, so Dizzy got up and pitched. He won the game, 6 to 2. But he was still not satisfied with the balk rule.

A short time later, in a speech at a banquet, Dizzy offered his opinion of the rule, of the men who had cooked it up, and of the league president who had ordered it enforced. That president was Ford Frick, an ex–newspaper writer whose specialty was, naturally, public relations — but not player relations. When Dizzy referred to Frick as "our great little president, but a pain in the neck to me," the head office took notice.

Soon afterward, an emissary arrived from Frick's office with a paper for Dizzy to sign. It was an apology to Frick and an acknowledgment that he understood the balk rule — plus an admission that he had deliberately thrown beanballs. Said Dizzy firmly:

"I ain't signing nothin'!"

Nor did he. Instead he went to a meeting at Frick's office, recited a few ready-made phrases, and was forgiven. But he was still angry over his treatment and hinted that he might not even play in the All-Star Game. It is too bad he did not stick to this resolve, for he did play in the game and it ended his career — not immediately, but within a very few seasons.

Dizzy, in the 1937 All-Star Game, was pitching to Earl Averill, the Cleveland slugger, when Earl smashed a ground ball right back at the mound. It struck Dizzy on the toe and caromed off into an infielder's hands. Earl was thrown out — but Dizzy was never the same again. Although his toe was broken, he stayed out only two weeks. He went back to pitching too soon, when he still had to favor the sore toe, and in doing so he changed his pitching motion. The result was an increasingly sore arm that became a chronic problem. He pitched two games before he felt something give in his arm, whereupon he himself predicted that he might be through for the season. But he came back after only a short rest, still limping, and was unable to produce a fastball. He won only 13 games that season, his last with Saint Louis. The following spring he was sold to the Chicago Cubs for $185,000.

When he started to pitch for Chicago, Dizzy knew his "fogger" (fastball) and his "crooky" were gone. But he still had his control and his knowledge of how to deal with hitters. Strictly on "cuteness," Dizzy won his first two games — even shutting out the Cardinals, 5 to 0, on four hits. Then he developed a kink in his arm and had to spend a month on the sidelines. When he came back, he was throwing sidearm but still managed to win ball games. He had five victories without a defeat. He even defeated the Pirates, 2 to 1, in the game that clinched the pennant for Chicago. He had won seven games that season and lost only one.

In the World Series, however, both his arm and his cuteness failed him. Pitching the second game, on a raw, windy day, Dizzy made it until the eighth inning, then fell apart and fed a home-run ball to Frank Crosetti, the Yankee shortstop. When Dizzy left the game the home fans rose up and gave him a mighty ovation — not for what he had done that day, but for what he had been through the past few seasons.

The next year, despite a weak, tired, and aching arm, Dizzy tried again and pitched six victories against four defeats. The year after that, 1940, Dizzy was shipped down to Tulsa to exercise his arm in the hot sun. He became a star in the Texas League, pitching sidearm and forgetting his fastball. He came back to Chicago in September to win two games there. In 1941, Dizzy still clung to hope that he might recover his power. He reported early, worked hard, pitched an inning against Pittsburgh and was knocked out of the box. He never pitched again in the National League. On "cut-down day," when the roster had to be reduced, Dizzy was signed as a coach.

He kept his coaching job two months and then moved into a job for which he seemed to have been trained from childhood: he became a sports broadcaster for a Saint Louis radio station. In this position Dizzy prospered, increased his fame, and won thousands of new fans, most of whom had never seen him win a ball game with his mighty arm.

True to his nature, Dizzy developed his own individual broadcasting style, bending the English language to fit whatever meaning he chose to put across. In Dizzy's world men "slud" to bases or "got throwed out." He forecast tactics and criticized strategy. "He's a gonna bunt!" he would shout without any ifs or buts. Or he would express dismay at a manager's decision.

Some people found Dizzy's casual attitude toward the canons of English usage more than a little distressing. One listener complained to the station that Dizzy set a bad example by his frequent use of the contraction *ain't*.

"Shucks," said Dizzy in response. "Everybody knows what *ain't* means!"

GEORGE HERMAN (BABE) RUTH

The One and Only

What is there left to say about Babe Ruth, after all that has been written about him already over the past quarter-century?

Everyone knows by now that he was, despite Roger Maris and Hank Aaron, the greatest home-run hitter who ever played in the major leagues. (Maris needed a longer schedule than Babe played to break Ruth's one-season record by one home run; and Hank Aaron required almost three thousand more times at bat than Babe before exceeding Ruth's career total.)

No one has yet come even close to Babe's career home-run average of 8½ percent — one homer in about every twelve times at bat. Nor has anyone ever managed to combine in one career home-run leadership and a collection of pitching records (one of which — number of scoreless World Series innings in a row — stood for many years). Ruth put in four seasons as a pitcher and for the better part of three of them he was the best or second-best left-handed pitcher in the American League.

THE BETTMANN ARCHIVE

Babe Ruth

He was an expert bunter, an aggressive and able base runner, a fine outfielder, and a good first baseman.

But even if he had not been all of that, he would still have been an extraordinary figure. For it was not merely his skills on the diamond that made Babe Ruth stand out in a crowd. He was a vibrant and dominating personality. In his youth, his jet-black hair, his lively eyes, the friendliness that beamed from his ruddy face, and his solid, trim, six-foot-two-inch frame would cause people to turn around and look at him. In any room he entered — even the Boston Red Sox locker room, when he was a youth just out of industrial school — he took command.

Nowadays, some people pretend to recall Babe Ruth as a sort of drunken bum, who spent much of his time brawling, drinking excessively, and living riotously through a short and misspent career. Babe Ruth was, it is true, a delinquent boy who never submitted entirely to discipline. He spent part of his childhood in a barroom, where his father worked; part of it on the shabbiest streets of Baltimore, where he became embroiled in all sorts of petty devilry; and most of it in a Catholic "home" for boys who needed some strict oversight. Even when he began to play baseball for money, he still behaved like a textbook bad boy, "borrowing" bicycles and even horses to ride until he grew tired of the sport, adorning all his speech with villainous profanity, and indulging in his appetite for good things to eat like a child turned loose in a candy factory.

But there is one point on which everyone who knew Babe Ruth as a youth will invariably agree: "Nobody," they will insist, *"nobody* disliked Babe Ruth." He might anger his mates on occasion with his outrageous practical jokes — like putting a piece of scorecard into somebody's lunchtime sandwich, or dropping a lighted cigar into somebody's pants as he was climbing into them. But he was one of the most openhearted souls who ever lived. No one ever had to ask him twice for a loan — often the money was given before it was asked for. Even when he was a small boy and saw dollar bills only when he snitched them out of his father's till, he would spend the money on buying ice cream and candy for all the kids on the street.

Babe, later on, did drink large quantities of beer at times, but he was seldom out of playing condition. He really damaged himself more by stuffing himself with great quantities of good food than he did by indulging in alcohol. He was never an alcoholic, and could abstain as long as need be if he found drink was affecting his play. "Hard stuff" — whiskey and gin — was just not his medicine. He sought gaiety, not oblivion, from drink, and no one ever saw him badly affected by liquor on the baseball diamond.

As for brawling, Babe never had any taste or any talent for that. He might bluster and threaten and offer punches in the nose, as all men in his circles did on occasion. But he very seldom exchanged blows with anyone — and when he did, he often came in second-best. Once, he and teammate Wally Pipp walloped each other while they were arguing over losing a ball game, but that exchange was over almost as soon as it started. Babe had four or five other fights in his career — far fewer than Ty Cobb had. And once — in Brooklyn, where Ruth served briefly as a coach — Burleigh Grimes, the big, tough pitcher, had to hold him off Leo Durocher, the one ballplayer Ruth truly despised. (Burleigh managed to handle both Babe and Leo at once.)

Most of the time, however, Babe was bubbling with good nature. He was delighted to have hero-worshiping kids around him and would wade in among them and join in their fun. No one could possibly record the number of visits he made to ill youngsters, or the charity appearances he made to help his old school or others like it. And surely no one ever matched the excitement Babe created among the young fans in a ball park. There was simply no anti-Ruth contingent among the kids — not in New York, or even Boston. And when kids got out of hand, as once they did at Yankee Stadium, a few shouts from the beloved Babe would line them all up and keep them in order.

Babe Ruth was noted, even when he was a pitcher, for hitting baseballs a long way. It must be remembered that, when Babe began to play in the big leagues, the ball was relatively dead and a dozen home runs in a season would most likely lead the league. Besides, fans were used to the Ty Cobb style of hitting — more of a push than a swing, with the idea of meeting the ball where it was pitched and placing it in safe ground. While Babe Ruth did not by any means introduce the cow-tail type of swinging — which involved unwinding fully and holding the bat at the extreme end (Babe used to curl his little finger under the knob) — he did repopularize it. And by illustrating the gate value of home runs, he prompted the manufacture of "livened-up" baseballs and the redesign of ball parks.

Babe, in his first training trip with the Baltimore club — which had signed him right out of industrial school — startled his coaches with his long, long blows. He was used then at first base, mostly to get some good out of his bat — but Babe was strictly a pitcher in his own mind. When he came up to the big leagues (with Boston), however, he was still trying to learn not to stick the tip of his tongue out of his mouth when he threw a curve — a habit that invariably told batters what to expect. At Providence, where the Red Sox placed him for some needed seasoning, Babe quickly hit a long home run in a game he was pitching and set the owners to considering his possible use as a pinch hitter when he was not on the mound.

Babe Ruth hit his first major-league home run in 1915, his first full season with the Red Sox, and he did it in a spectacular manner that should have foretold his future: he sent the ball screaming into the topmost rows of the right-field stands at the Polo Grounds, way up high where few were ever sent. Little note was made of that auspicious beginning in the press, however — although a New York sportswriter wrote that "Ruth was all a pitcher should be, and more," inasmuch as, in his first at bat, he drove the ball into the stands "with no apparent effort."

Ed Barrow, Boston's manager, was the man who gradually weaned Babe Ruth from the pitching mound and put him in the outfield to stay. Babe responded by hitting 11 home runs in 1918, to lead the league. (He also pitched in 20 games and won 13 of them.) The following season he developed into the greatest hitter in the league and began to acquire the fame that would turn his face into a trademark. He hit 29 home runs — breaking every record that the statisticians had been able to dig up, including one that went back to 1884 (27 home runs by Ned Williamson of the Chicago National League club); the "modern" major-league record of 24 home runs in a season had been held by Gavvy Cravath of the Phillies, who set it in 1915.

Yet Ruth earned his greatest fame not in Boston but in New York: Red Sox owner Harry Frazee, badly in need of cash to cover business debts, sold him to the Yankees. New York quickly became Babe's favorite playground (even though he retained a home in Massachusetts for a number of years). The Yankees built him "a stadium of his own," across the river from the Polo Grounds; and the lords of baseball helped along his career by adopting the ball that had proved so successful at boosting the batting averages in the short-lived Federal League — the lively "rabbit baseball," made to fly faster and farther off the bat.

In the 1920s, any sort of notoriety — even being convicted for staging a spectacular robbery — would earn a man a following of hundreds eager to slake their thirst for just a sip of fame. Babe's slugging accomplishments were real, honest, and repeated almost every day, so he quickly became a great celebrity. His personality was so naturally flamboyant and his ways so free that even the vulgarity of his manner (a throwback to his boyhood slum life), his barroom vocabulary (he actually did not know that some words he used in everyday conversation were deemed "dirty"), and his habit of making himself utterly at home in any surroundings did not lessen his popularity. Actually, in those days, newspaper writers seldom dissected the grimy details of an athlete's private life, so Babe's public personality remained about what it seemed on the surface — the image of an overgrown boy enjoying every second of a life that was full of home runs and cheering and easy money.

Babe, who could never school himself to wear underwear, bought silk shirts and neckties by the dozen. He owned a "thousand-dollar" leather coat and tried for a while to wear fedora hats, which just made his physically oversized head seem larger still. He had worn caps and sweaters in Boston, and he went back finally to wearing caps — when he wore any headgear at all off the diamond. He also bought himself an automobile with more cylinders in it than any other machine on the market. He was making $20,000 a year — millionaire money — and he was determined to enjoy every nickel of it.

It seemed for a time that Babe Ruth would just keep on hitting more and more home runs every year. The record-setting 29 had seemed incredible enough to the baseball fans in 1919. But Babe soon hit more than 50 in one season! And he predicted that, if he was able to keep from getting hurt, he would never miss a single game and would hit 75.

But Babe did miss a game now and then, even though he was always willing to play when he was injured. (It was a strange contradiction in Babe that, even though he would yell like a banshee when he knocked a finger out of joint, he would hurl himself into a slide regardless of bruises, bad knee, or injured elbow.) Once, Babe badly injured a toe when teammate Hal Janvrin, who had refused to take off an ancient top hat that Babe thought looked silly, set the hat on the grass with a rock under it; when Babe undertook to kick it into the adjoining township, the practical joke turned sour and Babe was put out of action for a while.

Babe never dogged it as some great stars have done — never went on strike or played sick to get out of a ball game. The worst fate that could befall Babe Ruth was being kept away from the park. (One day he was stopped for speeding on the way to the ball park and kept in jail during most of the game while the cops enjoyed his company.) Babe even played exhibition games in the South one time when he was running a very high fever: he refused to disappoint the crowds that had come to see him hit home runs. (He hit the home run they wanted, by the way, then the next day collapsed on a railway station platform.)

The amazing manner in which Babe outstripped all competition — to become, without question, "The One and Only" — is best indicated by the home-run figures in 1920, before the ball had been juiced up to allow almost every decent hitter to knock it half a mile. Babe hit 54 home runs that season. In second place, behind Babe, came George Sisler of the Saint Louis Browns — with 19. Cy Williams of the Phillies led the National League with 15. But even before Babe set his mark, he had astounded everyone in sight, a season earlier, with a spring-training home run that measured (according to a Boston sportswriter) 579 feet!

Babe simply did not believe that what he did in his off hours had any connection with his performance on the field. When he was with the Red Sox and had been caught creeping into his hotel room at six o'clock in the morning, a short suspension had scared him into temporary reform: he would do *anything* to avoid being kept out of a ball game! After he blossomed with the Yankees, however, and found doors opened for him wherever he turned, he assumed that ordinary rules were not meant for him. He sometimes got involved in celebrations that lasted all night long and hardly showed up in his hotel room *at all.* Eventually, his manager, Miller Huggins — who had been fretting over the matter for weeks as Babe's batting average dropped lower and lower — suspended the Babe and fined him $5000.

This set Babe Ruth to howling in rage and indignation. The *idea* of plastering such a fine on him — why that was more than they fined bootleggers! But the fine was not rescinded, despite Ruth's confident insistence that Colonel Jake Ruppert, the owner, would never permit it to stand. Ruppert not only permitted it, he endorsed it. Babe, as was his wont when he knew he was wrong, ultimately reversed his stance completely, apologized to everyone, including Huggins, and then struggled in agony for several days waiting to be allowed to play ball again. Babe shaped up and his batting average never again fell below .300 until he was thirty-nine years old, nine years later.

Of course, Babe did not completely reform — but he took care not to fall so far out of condition again that he could not hit a baseball safely three times out of nine or ten tries. Two years after the suspension, although many an expert had predicted he would never reach his peak again, Babe, in 1927, set the mark of 60 home runs in a season — the incredible record that stood until 1961 (when the longer schedule helped Maris set a new record with just one more homer than Babe had hit). Babe was thirty-two years old in 1927, and a long, long way from through: he hit 54 home runs the next season and at least 40 every year after that until 1932.

Babe Ruth's home runs were never freaky nor accidental. Although some people claim he chalked up some of his home runs cheaply — under the old rules, which made homers of balls that bounced into the stands — he never made a single one that way. In every park, he hit balls farther than any other player had ever hit them before. He occasionally smashed home runs completely over the grandstand roof at the Polo Grounds — and only "Shoeless Joe" Jackson had ever performed such a deed as that. Joe was one of the greatest hitters who ever lived, but Babe's home runs traveled even farther than Joe's did.

Of course, once the ball had been enlivened and batters had begun to swing hard rather than push or punch at the ball, other players, too, started to hit many home runs — forty or fifty or more in a season. But none of them ever replaced Babe Ruth as the standard of the mighty slugger — and none of them ever pretended he could. The name *Babe Ruth* was as famous as that of George Washington and was worth big money to Babe whenever he saw fit to attach it to some bit of merchandise or to back a commercial venture.

Fortune struck one candy maker who had, years before, named a chocolate bar *Baby Ruth* — after President Grover Cleveland's daughter. Kids suddenly began to clamor for this almost forgotten delicacy because they mistakenly believed it had been blessed by their baseball hero. Babe actually had invested, years before, in a small cigar factory in Massachusetts, and when he appeared for the first time in the Yankee spring-training camp, he was carrying a box of his special brand of dried and twisted weed, which he offered about to his new teammates (a few of whom suspected the things might be loaded). As for Babe himself, he arrived puffing on a priceless (though hideous) meerschaum pipe.

Babe was not often called "Babe" in the Yankee locker room, actually. He had been "Jidge" to the men on his club since his days in Boston — that being the New England diminutive for *George,* Babe's real monicker — and his teammates stuck with it. (He had been dubbed "Babe" in Baltimore by his first manager.)

An illness struck Babe during spring training in 1925 and led to an operation on his stomach for an abscess. At first it looked as if he might end up on the shelf for a season or two, but he was back on the diamond on the first of June — and back on the primrose path even before that. At other points he came down with "incipient influenza" (venereal disease) and other minor physical disabilities, or suffered disciplinary setbacks. (Once, he was suspended for the first few weeks of the season for ignoring a rule against postseason barnstorming.) In general, however, Babe played regularly and in good health, swinging a hefty bat even after his poor old legs, weary from years of carrying more weight than they were built for, had started to give way. In his final days with the Yankees — after he had been passed over in the search for a manager — he still was able to make a number of really sensational catches in the outfield. And he did the same after he had been shipped off to take an "assistant manager's" job with the Boston Braves.

With the Braves he one day put on a final spectacular show — one that really should have closed out his career, as a home run appropriately closed out Ted Williams's. Playing in a game against Pittsburgh at Forbes Field, Babe — whose waning abilities had been laughed at by the Pittsburgh pitching staff in their pregame clubhouse discussion of Boston batters — belted three terrifying home runs, two of them clean out of the ball park. And he hit them against three different pitchers, each one of whom had convinced himself that he knew exactly what pitch to feed Babe to lure him into a swing and a miss. Red Lucas offered Babe his high hard one — but Babe hit it higher and harder still: it sailed right over the right-field stand. (Many observers remarked that it was the longest home run they had ever seen in their lives.) Then Bill Swift fed Babe Ruth fastballs. Babe calmly launched one of those into the seats in center field. Finally Guy Bush, who knew the Ruth of old and also thought he knew precisely what was needed to get the old lion out, stepped to the mound. He got two quick strikes on the Babe with fastballs. Then he went into an exaggerated windup and flipped the old man the killer pitch — his dazzling fall-away sinker, which no man alive could hit safely. Babe promptly laid into it and sank it outside the park.

There were, alas, other, drearier, scenes before Babe finally resigned his job. "But I am not leaving baseball!" he vowed. And soon afterward, he put in an unhappy spell as "coach" of the Brooklyn Dodgers, where he still thought he might be made manager. Finally, he had to admit to himself that no one was going to hire him to manage in the majors. He did have an offer of a minor-league job, but Babe was not about to return to the bushes. Or he could easily have settled into a fairly pleasant routine of promoting amateur baseball — a cause to which he did devote much time — and quietly enjoying his wealth. (His resources derived to some extent now from conservative investments made for him when he was earning the then fantastic sum of $1000 — and at one point even $1600 — a week in baseball, plus even larger sums from a movie he made with comedian Harold Lloyd and from countless product endorsements.)

But the neuralgic pains he had been suffering in neck and arms turned out to be symptoms of cancer; his oversized body began to waste rapidly away. He soon could no longer play golf, a game to which he had become devoted once he had seen how far he could make the little ball travel when he hit it squarely. Babe still went traveling, though: to appear at benefits for American Legion baseball and other causes. He had always been an easy mark when asked to help young people, particularly young baseball players, and he accepted the burden of such invitations — even when he found it exhausting to move and almost impossible to talk — as if they were a religious obligation.

Babe appeared, too, at Yankee Stadium for an official farewell, in which he made a touching good-bye speech in the gravelly whisper that was all the disease had left of his voice. He heard then for the final time, and in overwhelming measure, the tidal roar of applause that swept down from the stands, which were filled to the final foot with men and women and children who had come to honor him for the miracles he had performed on the baseball diamond and the good deeds he had done off field all along the way. All the delinquencies of the once shabby little rowdy who had grown up to be the very embodiment of the National Game were finally forgiven: only the glowing happy face, the indomitable grin, and the booming chuckle that could set a whole room laughing seemed destined to be remembered.

LEROY (SATCHEL) PAIGE

Old Man Mose

When Satchel Paige entered the big leagues, as a pitcher with the Cleveland Indians in 1948, his age was supposed to be a secret and was reported in different newspapers as anywhere from fifty to "going on sixty-five." Yet all during this time his birth certificate was on file in Mobile, Alabama, and anyone who wanted to learn the true answer could have easily discovered he was merely a few months short of forty-two. He was born on July 7, 1906, and he stayed in the game long enough to be called "Old Man Mose."

Of course, most pitchers by the age of forty-two have turned to tending bar, tending their gardens, or tending to their grandchildren. But Satchel Paige, a black player who had almost thirty years of baseball behind him, had six seasons of major-league baseball ahead of him still. (His final "season," at the age of fifty-nine, consisted of three innings pitched for Kansas City, in which he struck out one batter and allowed but one hit and no runs.)

There is no question that Satchel Paige was one of the marvels of

NATIONAL BASEBALL HALL OF FAME

Satchel Paige

the century. When he still enjoyed all his youthful strength, Leroy Satchel Paige may well have been the fastest pitcher in the nation, or even in history. It was said that when he really poured a baseball in to the plate with his full strength, it might tear the glove off the catcher. When he finally arrived in the major leagues, he was able to get batters out, as he put it, by "outcuting" them. He had about a dozen different deliveries, so no batter alive could foretell at just what point in Satch's windup the ball might be released. He might step and throw, or throw and then step, or take an extra crank or two before letting the baseball fly. He was lean, strong, tireless, and mean — that is, like so many pitchers, he looked upon batters as enemies and used whatever methods he was allowed to get them out.

Leroy Paige became "Satchel" not because he had feet as big as suitcases (although when he raised his foot in a batter's face, the nervous batter might swear it obscured the sun), but because, as a working lad, he invented a device for carrying three or four satchels at once, so he could earn a dime apiece as a porter at the railroad station. His feet *were* big, though — size fourteen.

When Satch was young, he built strength in his pitching arm, as so many poor boys did, by throwing rocks. According to Satch — whose tales about his own prowess were not always to be believed — he could kill a chicken with a rock at thirty feet on the first throw. Just an inborn talent, he said. He also threw rocks in gang fights against white youths from a nearby school. In such instances he threw with extra power — not from any inborn talent, but from anger deeply ingrained by the humiliations a black child had to live with in the South.

Satch was ten years old when he started playing baseball with his school team. It was almost the only school activity that could hold his interest. Books just drove him to playing hooky, as they did many boys that age. But baseball consumed his soul. He loved to throw and he loved to hit and he seemed to do both equally well. He also, like many poor children, black or white, found it easy to get into trouble — for skipping school, for fighting, or for trying to snatch some of the goodies he could not afford to buy. When he was eleven years old — and already known about Mobile as the best kid pitcher in the schools thereabouts (in that day even the grammar schools fielded baseball teams) — Leroy was sent away to industrial school at Meigs, Georgia, after stealing some junk jewelry from a dime store.

Industrial school turned out to be a sort of haven for little Satch. At least it kept him well fed and disciplined, and gave him a chance to play baseball. (He also sang in the choir and played a drum in the bugle corps.) And he actually began to learn things from books. When he left the school he was well on the way to being a man and had already decided that his profession was going to be baseball. He stayed at the school until he was nearly eighteen, and by then had grown to his full height, almost six-foot-four.

Satch, along with his older brother, first played baseball for money with the Mobile Tigers, a black semipro team that played regularly in a fenced-in park. His pay was about a dollar a game, for which he pitched uncounted no-hitters. He also earned a few dollars helping out at the local minor-league park, where the white manager wished aloud — after watching Satch pitch in a "batting practice" in which nobody could hit the ball — that Satch were a white man so he could play in the league without violating the whites-only rule.

Regular paydays came to Satch when he moved to Chattanooga, Tennessee, to play for the Black Lookouts, an organized team with a league to play in and a regular payroll. Satch was paid $50 a month, plus a few dollars extra now and then when the manager slipped him a "bonus." He also picked up side money at the local pool hall — for he was as slick with a pool cue as he was with a baseball. As for his pitching, Satch allowed that he could "nip the frosting off a cake" with his fastball. He could indeed at least have knocked off the candles.

In two years with the Chattanooga club, Satch, as he recalled it, lost only two ball games. And before he was finished there, he was collecting $200 a month in salary.

Satch in the following years did a lot of hopping from one club to another, looking for better pay and bigger bonuses. He pitched for a while in New Orleans and then returned to Chattanooga. He moved to the Birmingham Black Barons for $275 a month. He had yet to learn how to throw a curve; his exquisite control and his incredible speed were all he needed to get batters out. He did have two ways of delivering his fastball — with fingers on the smooth skin of the ball and with fingers across the seams. The former was his "bee ball" and the latter was his "jump ball." The jump ball jumped, according to Satch, "from four to six inches." It surely looked that way to batters who kept swinging underneath it.

When he belonged to Birmingham, Satch used to be sent out on loan to other ball clubs, so his fame spread quickly to every corner of the South — and to part of the North as well. He was a favorite in Saint Louis, where he sent his new roadster roaring up and down the avenues and earned a hatful of speeding tickets. He also, like so many black players, very soon discovered Cuba — where baseball was played all winter, where black men could stay in decent hotels, and where paydays were steady. Satch also pitched and spread his fame in Venezuela and Puerto Rico. Back in the States, he played for the Nashville Elite Giants, who had bought his contract from Birmingham; the Elite Giants soon moved their operation to Cleveland, where gate receipts were fatter.

Satch's real fame developed — or rather his fame in the white world developed — when he signed with the Baltimore Black Sox to go on a postseason barnstorming tour with a team led by Babe Ruth. Satch pitched against some of the mightiest sluggers in the lily-white major leagues and left them all marveling. But he never had a chance to pitch against Babe Ruth, who seemed to be needed on the bench whenever Satch was scheduled to pitch. In a game on the West Coast, against the Babe Ruth All-Stars, Satch struck out twenty-two major-leaguers — and that would have been a new record in the major leagues.

The Nashville Elite Giants (they kept the name *Nashville* in Cleveland) breathed their last in the depression year of 1931 and Satch, like all his teammates, was cast adrift. But Satch was picked up almost instantly by the Pittsburgh Crawfords, the best black club in the country — the team on which one of the mightiest sluggers in all baseball, a catcher named Josh Gibson, first earned renown. (Gibson always felt — with much justification — that he, rather than Jack Robinson, should have been the first black player signed to play in the majors.) Other Crawford stars included Judy Johnson, perhaps the best-fielding third baseman alive when he was in his prime — a man who could move far to his left to take ground balls away from the shortstop, yet who could tightly close up the gap along the third-base line; and Oscar Charleston, still considered by men who played with him the hardest hitter in baseball — a line-drive slugger and expert fielder who could cover the entire outfield if need be, or, with equal ease, play close behind second base.

In his first game for the Crawfords against the Homestead Grays, who had "Smoky Joe" Williams on their side, Satch struck out sixteen batters. Soon afterward he met the girl he was to marry, a waitress at Gus Greenlee's Crawford Grill — home base for the club.

In Pittsburgh, Satch's salary jumped from $250 a month to $750 and he began to dress in keeping with this "millionaire" salary. In later life (like Babe Ruth, who toned down his outfits after dressing like a barber pole when he first began to draw big money), Satch's choice in clothes became tasteful and subdued. In the first flush of riches, however, Satch bought the loudest stuff he could find, delighting in his reputation as a flashy dude. But he always kept himself neat and clean — his suits tenderly brushed and pressed, his size-fourteen shoes gleaming, and his shirts without a spot.

With the Crawfords, Satch showed the way to big money for all the black stars. Wherever he appeared, with Josh Gibson as his battery mate, fans, both black and white, would nearly demolish the turnstiles to come see them pitch and catch and hit. Eventually the Crawfords had to begin to borrow major-league parks to hold all the customers. And salaries for the top black ballplayers began to read a little bit like those for the white players at the top of the major leagues.

It is doubtful, though, that the white players had as much fun as the black ones did, for the black promoters had to resort to fantastic stunts to keep the fans excited — since at first there were no pennant races to increase tension in the black leagues. Gus Greenlee, the Crawfords' owner, would hang up posters before a game announcing that Josh Gibson would *guarantee* to hit two home runs, at least, and that Satchel Paige would guarantee to strike out the first nine men. And the two battery mates would perform exactly as advertised. (Satch had another remarkable stunt he used to employ to keep his fans yelling: he would point to an infielder, designating *him* as the man who would make the next play, and would then see to it that the batter hit the ball to the selected fielder.)

Gus Greenlee became Satch's agent and signed him for exhibitions throughout the nation, and the extra paychecks soon set Satch to looking for new ways to spend his wealth. He owned the shiniest and longest cars a man could buy. He went in for trapshooting, at which he was as sharp a performer as he was on the mound, and he owned a collection of prize shotguns. He also collected lady friends, but he always came back to the girl he was going to marry, Janet Howard in Pittsburgh.

Satch continued to play ball throughout the Caribbean lands and traveled far and wide throughout the United States, facing scores of white major-leaguers. He won the respect of them all. Said Dizzy Dean, after a game against Satch's team: "If Satch and I were both on the same club, we'd have the pennant sewed up by the Fourth of July!" And Joe DiMaggio — who finally, after several vain tries, got a scratch hit off Satch's delivery — declared, "Now I *know* I can hit big-league pitching." (Joe was at the time still playing for the Seals in San Francisco in the Pacific Coast League.)

In 1934, Satch jumped out of his contract with the Pittsburgh Crawfords because, he said, Gus Greenlee refused him a raise. Satch had just got married and needed the steady money but was always ready to jump wherever the top dollar could be found. This time the top offer came from the "semipro" club in Bismarck, North Dakota. Satch did not discover until he arrived that the rest of the club was white. This circumstance did not really upset him — although some of his teammates were ready to rebel until they saw how Satch could pitch.

The Bismarck club, with Satch on the mound, did rebel against him one day, however — or at least the outfield did, stomping off the field after Satch had bawled them out for loafing. Satch — if you are to believe his recollection of the incident — merely pitched with no outfielders, and struck out the side!

After a lucrative barnstorming trip with a team of white all-stars headed by Dizzy Dean (who became his favorite barnstorming partner), Satch returned to play in Bismarck again the next year. This time there was a semipro invitational championship series set up in Wichita, Kansas, and Bismarck, with Satch's aid, won their way into it. In Wichita, Satch not only won all his games and the championship, he set a tournament record of sixty strikeouts in four games. He was named Most Valuable Player in the tournament — as if anyone needed to be reminded.

By the time Satch returned to the Crawfords, in 1931, there was talk everywhere of a possibility that the big leagues might let black players try out, but Satch himself had no real hope of it. As a matter of fact, he agreed with a few of the grumbling white players who said that "social angles" would prevent the integration of the leagues — that is, black players would be unable to share hotels and restaurants and perhaps even showers and locker rooms with whites.

In 1937, Satch jumped the Crawfords again to play for $30,000 in the Dominican Republic. (This was more money than the famed Dizzy Dean was earning.) He also jumped out of his marriage to Janet, began to avoid old friends from his semipro days, and spent his time pitching a few innings here and a few innings there for large fees. Money was coming in now almost faster than he could spend it and Satch began to put on airs, like a movie star. He made up with Gus Greenlee and the Crawfords just long enough to enjoy a few paydays, then took off for Mexico where dollars flowed more freely. Mexican food was not for Satch's stomach, however, and he often had "the miseries." He also, as a result of pitching every day, came up with a lame arm that seemed to mark the end of his career. It did mark the end, for a time, of his free spending.

Back in the States, Satch played first base with a barnstorming club until his arm recovered; then he joined the Kansas City Monarchs and started again on his merry-go-round of triumphs. Season after season he led the Monarchs to the championship, and in his spare time he hopped from one exhibition game to another, cashing in on his renewed fame. He used his off-diamond time to add to his collection of shotguns, antiques, and speeding tickets, while expanding his list of girlfriends. But his work was hard all the same, for he was constantly on the move, playing in all sorts of conditions — on fields with ups and downs like a cow pasture and under lights that left part of the outfield in darkness — traveling by bus, by plane, in his own car, and continually facing batters he had never seen before.

But he had a formula for dealing with all strange batters. "I just give them old number one," he explained. "My fastball."

In 1942, Satch pitched one of his best games. He was thirty-six years old and had admitted to himself that his "old number one" did not land in the catcher's glove with quite the zip it used to have. But at Wrigley Field in May of 1942, Satch worked for the Monarchs against the Dizzy Dean All-Stars — big-leaguers who had entered the armed services for the duration of the war. Before a crowd of almost thirty thousand, Satch pitched six innings and gave the big-leaguers just two unhealthy singles, both infield rollers (Satch fielded one himself, but the first baseman failed to cover the bag). After the game, Dizzy Dean allowed that if Satch were pitching in the majors he'd be "worth a million dollars."

The Monarchs hung on to old Satch until the call came for him to try out with the Cleveland club in the American League. Satch pitched Sundays for the Monarchs and weekdays almost anywhere the dollars beckoned. He kept count one year and said he pitched in 134 games — almost a full season's worth in the majors.

Satch was in Bremerton, Washington, in 1948 when an emissary from Bill Veeck, then owner of the Cleveland Indians, reached him. Satch, despite his oft-expressed opinion that a black player would be licked by the social angles in the big leagues, hesitated not even a half-second when Veeck's offer came. The deal was to be kept secret, so Satch sidled into town on the Fourth of July and told inquirers that he was looking for a job with the Cleveland Buckeyes of the Negro American League. But before the Buckeyes could type up a contract, Satch drove down to the Cleveland Stadium and began his tryout by loping part way around the park. Then he pitched to Lou Boudreau, the manager, who was not yet a Paige enthusiast. But Satchel threw fifty pitches to Boudreau and Lou counted forty-six strikes. Boudreau instantly adopted the Paige religion, and on July 7 old Satch signed a major-league contract.

Many sportswriters — particularly those who had been around long enough to have acquired "total wisdom" — were outraged that Veeck would stoop to such a cheap publicity stunt as signing a creaking ancient during a hot pennant race. There were already blacks on big-league clubs, but there were not many senior citizens. And Paige, according to the legends, was over fifty. But Paige offered to pay a $500 reward to anyone who could prove he had pitched a baseball game before 1927 (when he was twenty-one). A Cleveland fan immediately came up with a box score that showed Satch had pitched for the Chattanooga Black Lookouts in 1926, before he was twenty.

"I must have slept that year," said Satch, as he handed over the prize.

Satch pitched his first big-league game against the Saint Louis Browns on July 9, 1948. The umpire had to explain to him that pitchers in the big leagues were required to take the catcher's signal with one toe on the rubber. Satch pitched two innings, allowing two hits and no runs, before he retired happily to the showers. On July 14, he pitched an exhibition game against the Brooklyn Dodgers and worked four innings without giving up a run — and in one inning he struck out the side.

Altogether, in his first month with Cleveland, Satch pitched 26⅔ innings, struck out 16 batters, and allowed 7 earned runs. But he helped the club even more at the gate than he did on the mound, for when he was advertised as the pitcher, he drew over 70,000 fans in Cleveland. In Chicago, when his name was announced, the park was filled to the eaves and 10,000 were turned away after the turnstiles broke down.

In his second month, Satch began to feel at home. He shut out the White Sox on five hits in Chicago, then shut them out again in Cleveland 1 to 0, on three hits. On August 30 he beat Washington, 1 to 0. By the time the season was over and the Indians had beaten the Red

THE BETTMANN ARCHIVE

Satchel Paige relieving for the Cleveland Indians, 1948

Sox in the play-off game for the pennant, Satch had won six games and had lost one. His earned run average was 2.48.

Paige made a brief appearance in the World Series. In the fifth game, with the Indians clearly beaten (three Cleveland pitchers had already been bombed off the mound), Satch came in, pitched to two batters, and got them both out. He was replaced by a pinch hitter in the eighth and that was the end of Satch's World Series experience.

The Indians let Satch go in January 1950, after a season in which he won four games and lost seven. Officials in the big leagues had outlawed Satch's "hesitation" pitch and had thus robbed him of one of his best weapons. The umpires, for their part, had permitted the pitch, which simply involved Satch's throwing the ball *after* he had planted his forward foot in a stride toward the plate. But the president of the league, after listening to howls of anguish from victimized managers, looked at the pitch himself and called it illegal.

Satch's offhand attitude toward travel schedules had given his owners some uneasy moments. Sometimes, usually on a Sunday, he would oversleep (he had gotten married again, had started a family, and had become more of a fireside man). Once or twice he missed the train and had to "catch a bird" to bring him to the next town. Veeck, who had sold his interest in the Indians, had been patient with him. The new owners were not.

After a full year of barnstorming again, Satch returned to the big leagues in 1951, when Bill Veeck bought the Saint Louis Browns and signed him up. Satch also had offers from the New York Giants and the Boston Braves, who had scouting reports on his performance with the Chicago American Giants, his most recent club. But Satch preferred to work for Veeck, who had given him his first big-league job. Veeck's club was a hopeless collection and they had trouble — not only winning games, but drawing crowds, and even staying in the league. Satch worked hard for Saint Louis, pitching 62 innings and striking out 48 men. But his incredible stamina had begun to fade. Satch had had all his teeth extracted; he suffered from constant stomach woes and was past his forty-fifth birthday. And the team behind him had no Josh Gibsons or Oscar Charlestons to give Satch runs to work with. On exhibition tours with the Browns, Satch began to run into some hard-core racial prejudice — an obstacle that his new fame had almost caused him to forget. He was refused service in restaurants and ordered out of hotels. He spent a good many days in a froth of anger.

With Veeck still in charge, Satch signed with the Browns for 1952 and made it his comeback year. He won 12 games, saved 10 in relief, and struck out 91 batters, to help pull the Browns out of the cellar. Satch led the league in number of innings pitched in relief — 100. In tough spots, Veeck said, Satch could throw the ball as hard as any pitcher in the league.

In 1953, however, old Satch's "number one" had nearly deserted him. He blamed his new manager, Marty Marion, for ordering him to throw pitches he did not want to throw, and he complained constantly about his stomach. And he won just three ball games. In 1954, Veeck sold the club and the new owners moved it to Baltimore. They left old Satch behind.

Satch went back to barnstorming, pitching again in three or four games a week and covering the country from one corner to the other. Then Bill Veeck invited him to Miami to play for his minor-league Marlins, and Satch there found a league he could be a winner in again. As a matter of fact, he led the International League, with an earned run average of 1.86 — although his fiftieth birthday was long gone.

Satch had a falling out with the Miami management after Bill Veeck left. The new bosses were less tolerant about providing haphazard advances on salary and listening to excuses for missed planes. Still, Satch won more games than he lost and kept his earned run average down below 3.00. When the season was over, however, there seemed to be a mutual agreement that Satch would not return.

After that, Satch made a movie and returned to hopping about the country to make two- and three-inning appearances. In 1961 he signed with Portland of the Pacific Coast League and pitched 25 innings, in which he tallied 19 strikeouts. He was now fifty-five. In 1965, he made his brief appearance with Kansas City. His accumulated playing time made him nearly eligible for a big-league pension now, so Atlanta signed him as a coach, gave him a rocking chair to sit in, and let him pitch one inning in an exhibition against the minor-league Richmond club. Satch struck out the first two batters and got the third batter on an easy ground ball. Then he returned to his rocking chair. He was sixty-three years old.

Someone once wrote down a whole series of rules about life and baseball and ascribed them to Satch. But there was only one, Old Man Mose said, that he really went by: "Don't look back. Something may be gaining on you."

JACK ROOSEVELT (JACKIE) ROBINSON

First Black across the Line

Jackie Robinson's actual first name was not "John" but "Jack" (which is usually a nickname). And his middle name was given in honor of the Republican President Theodore Roosevelt rather than the more commonly honored President, Democrat Franklin Delano Roosevelt. In other ways too, Jack was an unusual man. He was primarily a football star at college, and it had never been his ambition to make his living at baseball. He was a proud, sensitive man who, one might think, would have been the very last person to have been able to school himself to accept racial insults as the price of breaking the obscene "color line" in the major leagues.

But Jackie had to do just that. He actually was required to submit to a sort of dress rehearsal in the office of the Brooklyn club owner, Branch Rickey, to make sure he could control his temper under severe provocation. These sessions weren't easy, for Jackie had a quick temper and was known to "talk back" to abusive opponents and fans. Rickey undertook to call him all the dirty names that might be hurled at him

Jackie Robinson

by spectators and rival players—and perhaps even by teammates—when Jackie started to play ball in the white man's preserve; "nigger" and "burrhead" were the least of them. Jackie boiled, but he did not boil over. He knew that it was important, not just to him but to the country, that this "experiment" of Rickey's should work out peaceably.

Branch Rickey, it was often said, brought Jackie into organized baseball out of plain, low-down greed for profits. This has been the motive for almost every major change in the game—especially for the shift of franchises from one city to another—and there indeed seems to be no reason to doubt that Rickey was clearly aware that he might improve gate receipts by signing Jackie. But, whatever the motivation, he had to buck a tightly organized and silent conspiracy to have his way, and he had to plan his move carefully and at length.

Although Jackie Robinson seemed like the product of a cultured middle-class home — well mannered, articulate, well educated, and well informed — he was actually a child of poverty, born to share-cropper parents in Cairo, Georgia. Before Jackie was two years old, however, his widowed mother, Molly, took him to Pasadena, California, where she earned a living by taking in washing. After a time, Molly Robinson had saved enough to buy a house big enough to hold several lodgers, whose rent supplemented the family income. Jackie sold newspapers and caddied for golfers to bring in extra money. In high school, at Muir Tech, Jackie starred in every sport he tried. His favorite was softball; his best was football. He played baseball, too, as well as basketball, and ran on the track team.

Jack's mother had planned for him to be a doctor, but he was too hooked on sports to dedicate himself to any other profession. His ambition was to be a coach, inasmuch as a black man could never make any real money playing either baseball or football or even pro basketball. His accomplishments on the high-school football team won Jack a scholarship at UCLA and while there he won All-America honors at halfback. In the summer he played for the Pasadena baseball team, state amateur champs. The army drafted Jackie before he could graduate from college, however, and he never returned to finish. He earned a commission in the army, working up from private, and playing a great deal of baseball. When his hitch was over he took a job at $100 a week with the Kansas City Monarchs baseball team.

Jackie was never really happy in the Negro league. He thought spring training was a farce and he was irritated by the lack of discipline that allowed ballplayers to stay out all night if they liked and to while the evenings away drinking. When the old Brooklyn catcher Clyde Sukeforth, an emissary from Branch Rickey, offered Jackie a ticket to go East and meet with Rickey himself, Jackie promptly threw aside his job and took the train to New York. Jackie thought he was going to be offered a job with the Brown Dodgers, a team in the Negro league Rickey was trying to organize. He was twenty-six years old, had only a few of his best years left, and was eager for a salary big enough and a job secure enough to allow him to get married.

When Branch Rickey told Jackie Robinson he was headed for the real Dodgers and that he would be the first black man in modern times to break into the big leagues, Jackie did not quite believe him. Jack from bitter experience knew the steep mountain of prejudice that faced a black man trying to find a place in the white world. Jackie and several other black players had already been "looked over" by a big-league club, the Boston Red Sox (who, as it turned out, were the last club in the majors to accept black athletes). Jackie, Sam Jethroe (centerfielder for the Cleveland Buckeyes), and Marvin Williams (second baseman for the Philadelphia Stars) had all gone to Fenway Park to demonstrate their skills to old Hugh Duffy, Red Sox coach and holder of the highest batting average ever posted in the National League.

The trio had had to wait in Boston two days before they were granted the tryout; then they were brought in along with about a dozen high-school kids who were also eager for a tryout. The black players were sent out to field the balls hit by the youngsters before they themselves were permitted to hit. When they were, Robinson knocked the first pitch out against the fence and lined out several more drives just as powerful. Jethroe and Williams also hit sharply. They all received a handshake and congratulations, plus good wishes, from Hugh Duffy—but nothing more was ever heard from the Sox. (It turned out that a local city councilman had threatened to have the club's Sunday permit revoked if they did not give black players a chance: this charade of a tryout was all the "chance" they ever received.)

But Rickey soon persuaded Jack he was really serious and that there was a job on the Montreal club awaiting him, with assurance of early advance to the Dodgers. What Jack did not know until later was that another black player — Roy Campanella, then a catcher for the Baltimore Elite Giants — had already been interviewed by Rickey; because Campy was convinced the job was on the *Brown* Dodgers, he had said he wasn't interested.

Jack, once he knew he was indeed headed for the big leagues, called his mother in California to tell her the news. On October 23, 1945, Jack was presented to the sportswriters in Montreal, and they were truly impressed. But the impression Jack made on International League fans was far more startling. In his first day on the job, playing against Jersey City in Roosevelt Stadium in that club's hometown, Jack got three singles and a home run. For Jack, this more than made up for what he had to suffer during spring training: Montreal's manager — Clay Hopper, a native southerner — had been obviously resentful of his presence; a few of his teammates had called him dirty names; and the town authorities in Sanford, Florida — where the Dodger organization's central training camp was located — having notified the club that no black players would be allowed to play on a white team in that town, had forced the Montreal club to shift its practice sessions to Daytona Beach.

Jackie ran into other problems that spring, too. Trying to throw hard before his muscles were really in shape, he developed a sore arm, and his hitting ability also left him at one point. Then, at an exhibition game in Deland, Florida — just when Jack seemed to be getting his batting eye back again — he was ordered off the field by a local cop who vowed that while he was on hand to stop it, no black men would play on the same field as whites.

But Jack survived it all, and he celebrated his arrival in the league by showing the hostile Jersey City fans a little of everything. After grounding out to short and collecting a park full of boos, Jack came up with two men on base and boomed a home run over the left-field fence. Next time up he reached first base on a bunt, stole second, and made it to third on the second baseman's error. On third base, Jack took an exceptionally long lead, prancing just outside the baseline and threatening to break for home. The pitcher started his windup, observed the daring lead, stopped his motion, and threw to third. The umpire called a balk and Jack trotted soberly home. (To hasten his acceptance in the big leagues, he had promised himself he would not taunt the opposition or rub in any of his triumphs.)

Next time at bat, Jack hit a single and stole second again. And he singled again when he came to bat in the next inning! When the game was over — Montreal won it, 14 to 1 — the Jersey City fans poured out of the stands and joyfully crowded around Jackie. Enemy or not, they were delighted with the performance he had put on and they wanted to shake his hand and slap his back. And Jackie, too, indeed felt happy on that first afternoon.

In Montreal Robinson soon became the precious hero of the French-speaking fans, who called him "Zha-kee" and cheered his every move. Elsewhere in the league, however, he ran into occasionally virulent prejudice. While the fans in Louisville bombarded him with frequent cries of "nigger!" and other far worse names, the most consistently foul-mouthed of all fans were the spectators in Syracuse, New York, who seemed to grow almost hysterical with rage at the sight of a black man on a team with whites. But Jackie, true to his promise to Branch Rickey, kept his mouth shut tight, never returned an insult, and swallowed all his anger — even when he found himself abruptly shut out of the hotel where the rest of the club was staying.

When the season was over, Jackie was leading the league in batting. His club had won the pennant and with it the right to meet Louisville in the Little World Series. In the opener, the Louisville fans gave Jackie a double dose of old-fashioned southern bigotry and Jackie, who thought he had grown hardened to their cries, tensed up, determined to get back at the hostile crowd by beating the hell out of the Louisville club. But the harder he tried, the more ineffective he was at the plate — and the worse he looked at the plate, the wilder and more vicious became the cries from the stands.

But once the series had moved to Montreal, the tables were turned. The Montreal fans had made up their minds that the Louisville players would pay for the way their supporters had treated Jackie, so they nearly drowned the Louisville batters in boos and catcalls each time one of them approached the plate. And when Jackie came to bat, even if he just ticked the ball, the fans would scream in admiration and delight: "Zha-kee! Zha-kee!"

In Louisville Jackie had batted a feeble .200; at home in Montreal he batted .400. Montreal was down two games when they came home. But with Jackie at his best, they won all three games — and the championship — before the hometown fans. When the final game was over, the whole cheering mob descended on Jackie, lifted him high, and, along with manager Clay Hopper and pitcher Curt Davis, paraded the men around the park on their shoulders. Then they serenaded Jackie with the French version of "For He's a Jolly Good Fellow!" — a song called *"Il a Gagné Ses Epaulettes!"* Jackie, who had kept his emotions in check all season, stood on the field and wept.

Eventually, he bade everyone good-bye and started for the clubhouse to get into his traveling clothes and dash for the plane that was to take him home. But when he had showered and dressed, he opened the clubhouse door to find the runway packed full of excited French-Canadians gathered to embrace him. He gave his suitcase to a friend and tried to wriggle through. No use: *everyone* wanted to clasp Jackie in his arms or kiss his cheeks. So at last poor Jackie had to put one shoulder down and buck his way clear.

Once in the open, Jackie broke into a dead run, with a yelling pack of fans at his heels. It was like the beginning of a race riot, except that the mob was bent not on stringing Jackie to a lamppost, but on hugging him, shaking his hand, and kissing him good-bye. As Jackie sped down the street, hotels and restaurants emptied out and hundreds more joined in the pursuit. Finally, a man in an automobile stopped and gave Jackie a ride to his hotel. After Jackie had caught his breath and looked back over the event, he vowed: "I don't care if I *never* go to the majors. This is paradise!" And although he soon realized that he did not *really* mean it, he would often stop and recall that wild scene in Montreal. "It was the greatest thing that ever happened to me," he would say.

Of course, the whole purpose of Jackie's playing in Montreal was to prepare for the major leagues. The very next spring, Branch Rickey decided Jackie was ready to come up to the parent club. (First, however, he would have to learn to play first base, because that was the only spot on the varsity where there was room to put him.) As it became clear that Jackie was *really* going to play in Brooklyn — that he had not, as some sportswriters originally predicted, been so embarrassed and uncomfortable in his crusading role that he would quit of his own accord — there were rumblings in the league, from top to bottom. Before Jackie was signed, the club owners, meeting in solemn conclave, passed around for consideration a resolution — marked "for eyes only" (not to be talked about or reported to the press) — to the effect that signing a Negro player was a threat to the interests of organized baseball and to the property values so tenderly cultivated by baseball's financial backers. Afterwards, not a soul could be found — except for Branch Rickey — who would admit that such a declaration had ever been circulated. Said Rickey: "I'd like to see the color of the eyes of any man who denies that he saw that paper." Some did deny it, although they would not look Branch Rickey in the eyes when they made the denial. Anyway, what did happen was that the baseball commissioner, "Happy" Chandler, told Rickey to ignore the resolution and go ahead and sign Jackie to a contract.

Among the white players there was much grumbling and even some open rebellion. A few sportswriters — those who treasured their own bigotry as if it were a symbol of manhood — encouraged the rebellious players to take a stand against letting Jackie play. Finally, the Saint Louis Cardinals — or a good many of them — along with one or two on the Brooklyn club, agreed that they would go on strike if Jackie were to take the field in a league game in which they were involved.

Again, no one would ever openly admit later that there had been any strike talk at all — or, if there had been, that he had personally been involved in any way. But Ford Frick, president of the National League, issued a statement that must have been prompted by *something*. It certainly was a clear, courageous, and unequivocal assurance that any player who carried out such a strike threat was going to be out of a pro baseball job for life.

"I don't care if half the league strikes," the statement read. "Those who do it will encounter quick retribution. All will be suspended and I don't care if it wrecks the National Leagues. This is the United States of America . . ."

It was remarkable how this simple, incisive statement struck all the rebels dumb and set a number of the most earnest agitators to pretending that they had never even dreamed of rebelling — that indeed, they were all *for* Robinson. A few of the supposed ringleaders took special pains to be seen in friendly conversation with Jackie.

Jackie himself had trouble getting his stride in the big leagues, what with learning a new position and seeing a lot of hard throwing at the plate. He also received many an extra-hard tag from intolerant infielders eager to express their disapproval of Jackie's skin tone. Public pressure dictated that he could not be housed with his white colleagues in some cities, and he took his meals by himself. Even those of his teammates who were "friendly" to him sometimes revealed their contempt (and their ignorance) in alarming ways. One pitcher, rising from a card game in which he had had a bad turn of luck, walked back a few seats in the Pullman and — to "change his luck" — quickly rubbed his hand on Jackie's head. Even Branch Rickey could not explain how Jackie, straining with impatient rage, managed to keep himself from rising up to destroy the man.

The Philadelphia club — especially manager Ben Chapman, its renowned bench jockey — devoted a good deal of energy to calling Jackie the dirtiest names they could invent. So virulent did this abuse become that the commissioner of baseball had to shut Chapman's mouth for him with a stern rebuke.

But Jackie hung on despite constant harassment and at last began to lift his batting average. In June he started on a twenty-one-game hitting streak. On June 24, against Pittsburgh, he stole home. The team now began to accept Jackie as a valuable contributor and he was able to relax with most of his teammates — at least on the bench and the ball field. Elsewhere around the league he found other white players who were pleased to make friends with him and who offered him advice and encouragement. And Jackie himself sometimes defused the resentment that his treatment by hostile opponents began to arouse among his mates. When Enos Slaughter of the Cardinals spiked Jackie while running out a ground ball at first, Jackie urged his fellow Dodgers, who were talking of revenge, to cool it. He speculated that perhaps he had blocked too much of the bag: maybe the spiking had been accidental. Anyway, he pointed out, the white players sometimes got bumped too, but nobody made a federal case of it.

At the end of the 1947 season, Jackie had a batting average of .297 and led the league with twenty-nine stolen bases (he stole home three times). He was named Rookie of the Year by *The Sporting News,* and there was hardly anyone in the game who did not agree he deserved the title.

The next season, Jackie felt secure in his job and thus decided he had been released from his promise to Branch Rickey to hold his tongue under all provocation. He began to react to insult and abuse the way white players always reacted. And he dared to disagree out loud with umpires. He even joked about being kicked out of one game for talking back: two white players were ejected too, and that, Jackie figured, made him "one of the boys."

Although Jackie was given much credit for helping send the Dodgers into the World Series in 1947, his best season was actually 1949, when he won the Most Valuable Player Award and earned his best seasonal batting average: .342. One reason for his improved play that year, Jackie said later, was his ability to let off steam whenever he wanted. For instance, when one teammate tried to give Jackie the "darky treatment" during spring training, Jackie freely responded with epithets deemed improper for black men to use on their white "superiors" in the South in those days. And when ex-Dodger manager Leo Durocher, renowned for finding words and gestures designed to drive opponents into frothing fits of anger, tauntingly gave Jackie the "swelled-head sign" (he held one hand on each side of his head, as if grasping a pumpkin), Jackie retaliated. He turned so sharp a tongue on Leo — asking

BROWN BROTHERS

Jackie safe at third in a game against the Saint Louis Cardinals

him, for one thing, if he was still using Laraine Day's perfume (she was Leo's movie actress wife) — that Leo utterly lost his own cool and set out to throw punches at Jackie. That enterprise would undoubtedly have landed Leo on the deck, but fortunately other players held the two apart.

There were still umpires in the league who resented the very presence of black players in "their" game, and they were irritated beyond reason when Jackie began to react to their calls just as white ballplayers did. Although ejection from a game is supposed to be the umpire's last resort — to put an end to persistent abuse, to penalize outrageous language, to punish a player for striking, bumping, or making a violent gesture toward an ump, or to retaliate when a player indulges in throwing bats or other equipment — Jackie was kicked out of one game for merely giving an umpire the "choke-up" gesture that is commonplace on the diamond. And other umpires seemed to grow excessively long, sensitive ears when Jackie walked off growling his disappointment at a decision. On one occasion, according to Jackie, a conspiring umpire, overhearing what Jackie was muttering about another ump, repeated the words to his ridiculed partner and got Jackie ejected.

But in 1949, such episodes, although stirring Jackie's deepest rage, somehow seemed to have the same effect on him that anger had on Ty Cobb: they just made him play harder. (Connie Mack always used to warn his players, "Don't make Mr. Cobb angry!")

While it was still, in Jackie's day, difficult to find a hotel — especially in the South — where black players could stay with whites, and though it was impossible sometimes for a black ballplayer to get his hair cut even in the same town with his teammates, life rapidly grew more comfortable for the blacks who now began to fill the big-league rosters. Sympathetic white players began to walk out of restaurants that would not serve *all* the team members. Ball clubs refused to patronize hotels that tried to maintain racial segregation. And everyone associated with baseball, except for a few of the bigoted club owners and some of their pet sportswriters, learned to avoid demeaning terms like *nigger* and *coon* and *burrhead* when talking of blacks. So Jackie had in effect started an educational program, and as well as restoring decency, he brought back some of the elementary excitement to baseball with his aggressive baserunning.

Starting as late as he did, Jackie was wearing an aging veteran's arms and legs by the time he had completed but five seasons in the majors. His hair had begun to go gray and he no longer could get off to a catlike start from first base on his way to second. But he remained a strong gate attraction everywhere his club traveled and, while the nasty letters and name-calling did not entirely cease, they dwindled to the extent that Jackie could laugh at them. He was still a "show-off" and a "big-head" to some obstinate fans, who preferred black men who "knew their place." But he was a hero to nearly all the fans in Brooklyn. And he was a hero to many a small sick child who benefited from his attention or his charity.

Pitchers began to throw at Jackie in 1951, dumping him in the dirt a dozen times and once even stinging him in the ribs — but not because he was black: he was hitting the ball at a frightening pace and pitchers everywhere were trying to keep him from digging in at the plate. And Jackie retaliated in traditional ways — such as by laying a bunt down on the first-base line, where the pitcher had to field it, then bumping the hurler off the line with the full weight of his hard body. He also complained out loud, where writers could hear and report it, that there was altogether too much throwing at batters and that the league authorities ought to stop it.

Such public fault-finding irritated some of the game's spokesmen. *The Sporting News* and other publications called on Jackie to hold his tongue and to become once more a "credit to his race." But Jackie knew he belonged to the *human* race, and he was determined to behave as any normal human would who was having baseballs thrown at his head. The Dodger management publicly supported him and so did his mates. But one nut in Cincinnati acted on an urge to send Jackie an anonymous note threatening to shoot him when he took the field against the Reds. Jackie laughed at that one, especially when one of the Dodgers suggested that each team member wear a *42* (Jackie's uniform number) on his back, so the gunman would not know which player to pick off.

At the end of 1956, when Jackie was thirty-eight years old, his contract was sold to the Dodgers' dearest enemies — the New York Giants. By this time Jackie had begun to find that each season's aches and pains did not wear off as they once had. And, having "grown up" in Brooklyn — to which he had become as devoted as he had once been to Montreal — Jackie had no stomach for readjusting and forming allegiance to the Giants, a gang that had so long seemed dedicated to inflicting misery on him. So he retired from baseball and accepted a television job, while giving nearly all his spare time to public service. Jackie Robinson remained a man determined not to be pushed around by a hostile world, and he continued to live in comfort and dignity until his death in 1972.

THEODORE SAMUELS (TED) WILLIAMS

Doctor of Hitting

There was probably never a man in professional baseball who devoted to the art of hitting so much intense study and untiring practice as Ted Williams did. There have been dedicated batters like Rogers Hornsby, who would never attend a movie lest it disturb the acuity of his vision, and there have been disciplined players like Cap Anson, who never ate more than bread and milk for supper lest he grow too fat to hammer a baseball hard. But so far as anyone knows, no other hitter who succeeded in the big leagues ever put in the hours of meticulous practice Ted did: swinging a bat; taking aim at a baseball; examining his batting swing in a mirror; wielding an imaginary bat while he was supposed to be playing the outfield; timing pitches while he waited in the on-deck circle; questioning other batters about methods; delicately weighing bats, honing them, inspecting them, nursing them, assessing their balance; trying out new stances and different swings.

Ted Williams

Surprisingly, when he first started playing baseball, Ted set out to be a pitcher, and he acquired skill enough at that art to pitch two innings of major-league ball (during which he struck out the mighty Rudy York with a sidearm curve). Pitchers, however, did not play ball every day in the leagues, and Ted could never tolerate long stretches on the sidelines. Besides, hitting the ball — as all pitchers know — is really the most fun in the game. It is also, according to Ted, the most difficult job in all sports and thus requires the most patient study. One reason today's batters generally do not hit with such high averages as the great sluggers of the past, Ted believes, is that they just do not have the long stretches of quiet travel time in which to discuss batting and study its fine points.

Ted would talk batting to anybody who knew the least bit about the subject. When he saw a batter who could do something at bat that he could not do, he would experimentally imitate the man's methods for a while, and perhaps even adopt some small part of the man's stance or swing if it helped. Ted never reached the point where he thought he could not improve his hitting abilities.

Like Mickey Mantle — the great Yankee slugger who was similar in many ways — Ted Williams spent most of his childhood playtime in batting games — not baseball games, but just games between himself and a kid pitcher — so he was at bat all day long, off and on. And that is just the kind of training required to turn a man into a good hitter, for no one comes to bat often enough in a regular game to get even one-tenth of the practice he must have.

Ted also worried about his strength and worked to improve it. He was an exceptionally skinny boy. Even when he had fully matured and had entered organized baseball, he was inordinately thin — so much so that people would invariably remark on it. He was three inches over six feet tall, yet weighed barely 170 pounds. In high school, he was the same height but weighed only 145!

When he was a kid, Ted decided to strengthen his hitting muscles by doing pushups (Mickey Mantle built his up by swinging a sledgehammer in a mine). Pushups became a daily ritual with Ted for the rest of his life — as many as a hundred, on his fingertips. This sort of exercise strengthened his hands, too, until he was able to squeeze a bat so fiercely he seemed likely to wring juice out of it. And he played baseball six days a week, all year around.

Ted played the outfield well and pitched successfully for his high-school team, but even in those days everyone talked about his hitting.

He hit baseballs farther than any kid had ever hit them in San Diego — and perhaps in the whole state of California. His first chance to play for money came when a man who ran a liquor store offered him five dollars a day to play on Sundays for the ball club the liquor outlet sponsored. Ted's mother, a teetotaler and Salvation Army lassie, refused to let him play for so "sinful" a man, but Ted still played wherever he could. Even big-league scouts soon came to see this skinny kid who had been knocking baseballs out of the park. Eventually, though, Ted signed to pitch and pinch hit for the local minor-league club, the San Diego Padres of the Pacific Coast League.

Ted set no records with the Padres, but he did impress the scout for the Boston Red Sox, who signed him for a $1000 bonus — paid to Ted's mother, who had at first asked the Padres' manager not to sell Ted to the big leagues until he was twenty-one. Ted was not yet nineteen when he made his first trip to the Red Sox camp in 1937. He had to borrow money from a bank to make the trip.

The Red Sox assigned Ted to Minneapolis, where he began to hit the ball so freely and so far that he felt he had landed in paradise. But it was just a kid's vision of paradise — and Ted was one of the most unsophisticated kids in the world. Suffering from a basic shyness that he sometimes covered up with an almost breathtaking cockiness and a tendency to respond to even the mildest criticism with a nasty remark, Ted had some trouble at the start staying on good terms with his manager. But the manager, the old Detroit shortstop Donie Bush, quickly learned how to deal with Ted — how to soothe his tantrums and ignore his fresh mouth — and he got a great deal of good hitting out of his young prize.

But Donie did not get much good fielding. Ted had the markings of a fine outfielder; he seldom lost a ball he got his hands on, and he could throw a ball to third base from deep right field and put it right

NATIONAL BASEBALL HALL OF FAME

Ted at the plate

on the bag. But there were too many distractions in the outfield and too much time for Ted to celebrate the hits he had just made or the hits he was about to make. Ted used to trade jokes with the fans in the nearby seats and would sit down on the grass occasionally to watch the game from afar, almost as if he were not in it. When he had to gallop after a fly ball he would slap himself on the seat of the pants, like a kid playing cowboy, and yell "Hi-Yo Silver!"

The fans loved these antics, but Donie Bush thought for a time that this skinny, unbroken colt was going to drive him clear out of the league. One time Ted became so engaged in conversation with a fan that he never noticed a fly ball coming his way until the centerfielder almost knocked him down charging into right to try to catch the ball himself. One day Ted nearly ended his own career: in a fit of self-disgust after a failure at bat, he smashed his hand into a water cooler. Another time, upset with his hitting performance, he stalked right to the dressing room and had almost got into his street clothes when he was reminded it was his turn at bat.

One reason for Ted's frequent tantrums (he and Mickey Mantle both, on occasion, used to destroy nearby furniture or towels when angry), was that he demanded much more of himself than most players did. Every trip to the plate was, to Ted, like a visit to an unexplored planet. He had new things to discover about the pitcher, who might be throwing differently today from the way he pitched last time. There were points for Ted to bear in mind about his swing, especially if he had some new bit of advice to test. And often there was a definite goal in his mind concerning where he would like to send the ball. If he failed to wait for a certain pitch as he meant to, if he caught himself guessing wrong in anticipating a curve or a fastball, if he undercut the ball more than he intended — any one of these misdemeanors might send him back to the bench snarling at himself, and warning himself in disgust that he'd better *remember* next time.

Except for hunting and fishing (to which he devoted much of his time off) and movies — he loved them and sometimes went alone two or three times a day — Ted had practically no interest but baseball. He did not play cards. He did not smoke or drink. Late hours distressed him, as did late meals. He constantly pestered other hitters for information and advice: How did you deal with this pitch or that? How heavy a bat do you use? How can I improve my batting stance?

His batting seemed to improve all by itself — although there is no question Ted's tireless planning and practice accomplished the improvement — while the information he gathered about pitchers and pitching patterns began to render him nearly invincible at the plate. His tantrums behind him, his goof-offs forgiven, Ted pranced through his minor-league career like a kid turned loose on a sunny beach. He would wake up in the morning and do a jig on the bed, rejoicing in the arrival of each new day because it meant he could drive more baseballs out of sight. He swung rolled-up newspapers or blankets or magazines, pretending they were bats, and watched in the mirror to see if he looked right as he swatted imaginary baseballs into the glass. (Once, with a fierce swipe at a baseball that wasn't there, he knocked the bedstead right out from under his sleeping roommate.)

Supplementing all this were the endless hours of steadfast devotion when Ted had practiced hitting as a boy: lugging his bat to school with him daily; bribing other lads to fetch baseballs he hit out of reach; suffering blisters on both hands; passing up enjoyments such as going out with girls or seeking a taste of wild excitement with his buddies over the Mexican border — just hitting and hitting and hitting.

At the end of the 1938 season, when Ted had just turned twenty, he led the American Association in batting (.366), in home runs (43), in runs batted in (142), and in runs scored (130). There was no question he was going to move up to the big leagues immediately.

The 1940 Red Sox were overloaded with temperamental players — great stars of the thirties who had been sold off to Tom Yawkey's Red Sox as they began to grow a little white in the eye. Each one felt equipped to manage the team on his own, and one or two tried. One pitcher did not care to pitch when his astrology chart warned of disaster. Another would go into such fits of gloom after losing a game that Joe Cronin, the manager, feared he might attempt suicide and actually assigned a man to keep an eye on him. One Sox infielder would sometimes quit playing if the boss found fault with him. Another might appear in the locker room with a hangover almost too heavy to lug — and ready to fight any man who said boo. And one outfielder, who was hitting .340, was so given to second-guessing the manager at the top of his voice that he was shipped away to make room for Ted Williams.

Into this gang of bellyachers and soreheads and kooks came joyful Ted Williams, ready to tear the American League wide open, just as he had dismembered the American Association. Ted did not cavort quite so childishly as he had in Minneapolis: he did not smash any water coolers or tear up any towels; nor did he ever turn his back on the diamond to discuss the progress of a ball game with a fan. What he did do, after a wobbly start, was hit some of the most hair-raising home runs ever knocked out of Fenway Park. He thereby became the idol of the fans, and Ted seemed to love all the fans in return. When the crowd greeted a home run with a standing ovation, Ted would pluck his cap by the button and lift it as high above his head as he could reach, grinning so happily he seemed about to burst.

In his first seasons in Boston, Ted was anything but the glum, anti-social monster the local sportswriters in later seasons seemed to find him. He was naive, uninhibited, openhanded, and openhearted. He did indeed have moments of despair, when he would think of packing it all in and going back to California, and moments of rage, when he would seem about to destroy everything breakable within reach. He talked back to his betters, addressed manager Joe Cronin as "sport," and made a close friend of Johnny Orlando, the clubhouse "boy." He also made friends with a few hundred kids around Fenway Park, whom he would collect into a gang now and then to go with him to Revere Beach and ride the roller coaster — where Ted would have as much fun and yell as happily as anyone. Sometimes, he would hire transportation and enough tackle to take all the Fenway Park grounds keepers and clubhouse crew fishing with him; and Ted, of course, treated them all to food and drink.

Yet generous Ted was not earning the sort of money that would prompt the average ballplayer to start throwing his cash around. He was being paid about $10,000 — a good deal less than a run-of-the-mill advertising salesman could make in that day. But Ted never knew the value of a dollar the way a tightfisted Yankee shopkeeper might know it. Money was for fun, Ted had learned in his youth — and fun was sharing good times with other kids. (When he was in school, Ted even used to give away his lunch money to friends who had none.)

But the other side of Ted's boyishness was his incredible show of sulking when his performance did not meet up to his standards. Once, having been robbed of a seemingly certain home run by an unbelievable running catch (Elmer Valo, the culprit, banged into the bleacher rail so hard he had to be carried from the field), Ted, his next time up, just pushed his bat at the pitches with one hand; he finally dribbled a ground ball toward the second baseman but made hardly a pretense of running it out. On a previous occasion, Ted alarmed his manager by actually disappearing from the field between innings — he had stepped through a door leading to the scoreboard to check on the news from other ball parks and had stayed a little too long. Another time, when he hit a pop-up instead of the long drive he was always looking for, Ted merely rambled down the baseline, hanging his head and never noticed — until too late, after he had been put out — that his blooper had dropped in when the fielders could not decide who was to catch it and he could have reached first base safely. Cronin took Ted out of the game for that blunder, and the fans made unfriendly noises. (Soon afterward, Ted demonstrated his contrition by running madly to first on a weak tap back to the pitcher's mound; the fans laughed and cheered.)

Whatever Ted may have said himself, there is no doubt that concentration on his personal accomplishments at times interfered with his devotion to winning the ball game at hand. When it became clear that a glimmering chance to win the treasured Triple Crown — league leadership in batting average, runs batted in, and home runs — had eluded him one season, Ted's performance deteriorated and he exhibited utter indifference, even at the plate. He occasionally tried to "get even" with the fans, who yelled obscene and vicious insults from the nearby stands, by deliberately stalling — sometimes even allowing runs to score while he delayed returning a ball to the infield. But Ted would also spasmodically show his penitence by throwing himself into a play without regard for injury.

In 1941, Ted's third season with the Red Sox, he set a major-league record with a batting average .406 — the last time to date that anyone has exceeded the .400 mark. In going for that mark, Ted played his heart out all year, but at the end of the season he nevertheless refused to take a few days off to protect his average. He was not going to "back into" the record by refusing to take risks; he wanted to earn it at the plate — and he did.

The last two games of the season were played on a dank, chilly day in Philadelphia, as a doubleheader. When Ted showed up at the plate, the opposition players — and even the umpire! — were rooting for him to break the record. (The Philadelphia catcher, however, warned Ted that Philly manager Connie Mack had promised to suspend any player who eased up on Williams.) Bill McGowan, the umpire, took time out to dust off the plate and — without looking at Ted, apparently just talking to himself — muttered that "to hit four hundred, a man has to stay loose!"

Ted was loose: He hit a single. Then he hit a home run. Then he hit two more singles. In the second game he hit a double. He made six hits in eight times at bat and easily set his record.

Many of Ted's difficulties were rooted in his differences with the Boston sportswriters, all of whom at that time were straining for stories that would make headlines for their papers — and a few of whom had personal vendettas with Ted. One especially sour-natured character actually tried to strike at Ted by reporting that he "did not even go to see his mother" when the season was over. Why a sports analyst should be concerned with whether a player went to see his mother was not made clear. Besides, many other players failed to see their parents in the off-season. (Some of Babe Ruth's teammates never knew he *had* a mother, or a father either, because he never talked of either one and saw them hardly at all.)

But Ted was branded an ingrate and an unnatural son because he preferred not to return to the unhappy, untidy household where as a child he had often sat waiting during long, lonely evenings for his mother to come home. When Ted's first child was born, prematurely, some writers made headlines of the fact that Ted was far from his wife's bedside. One paper even took a sidewalk poll to dig up unfavorable "fan reaction" to Ted's failure to pace the waiting room awaiting the baby's birth.

Earlier, young Ted, innocently thinking he was talking confidentially to a friend, said something to a reporter about how much fun it would be to be a fireman. The remark was soon repeated nationwide in an embarrassing context. Enemy ballplayers clanged fire bells and wore firemen's hats to taunt Ted into a frenzy. He swore he would never trust a newsman again. (Years later, however, Ted made a similar mistake when he spoke of "gutless draft boards" who feared to defer athletes like himself who were obviously unfit for service, and of gutless leaders who were afraid to fight a war to win. The reporter, who, to Ted, had seemed too drunk to register what was being said, repeated every word. Ted was angry, but he did not retract a syllable.)

Ted was criticized frequently for not being one of the boys. He skipped out of the clubhouse before the champagne bottles were opened to celebrate winning the 1946 pennant, leaving before the reporters had a chance to ask questions. He just wanted to get back to his hotel room and start tying fishing flies — a hobby that gripped him like an addiction. Ted did not share his teammates' devotion to nightlife or cards, and he had his own friends — some of them too unfashionable to appeal to the tastes of his hotshot teammates. Babe Ruth, too, had his own pet retreat for drinking and eating away from ballplayers, but he was never deemed antisocial on that account.

Ted, when some special cause was at stake, would break bones for the sake of victory. He specialized in outdoing himself at All-Star Games and assuredly damaged his own career by playing on with an injury he received while fielding a fly ball against the wall in one such contest. He was ridden hard by both the press and his employers because he sought a draft deferment because of his dependent mother. (Other star players also sought special treatment, either deferment or cushy assignments, and received it — but without headlines.) But when Ted was called to serve in the Korean War, despite hearing ailments and a sore arm, which were more than enough to put another man on the shelf, he did his job heroically and nearly lost his life in the process.

And while Ted did at times make "obscene gestures" at fans and sometimes refused to acknowledge applause, he did show the fans what they paid to see — the greatest hitting of his era and perhaps of the whole century. Managers of other clubs devised special ways to try shutting off the flow of base hits from Ted's bat. Lou Boudreau, field leader in Cleveland, put most of his infield on the right side of the diamond, leaving no room for long drives off Williams's bat to drop safely. And Ty Cobb found fault with Ted for not "hitting to left" (although Ted once got two home runs over the left-field fence in the same game). But then, nitpickers had criticized the great Babe Ruth, too — for not bunting for base hits!

Had it not been for the interruptions in his career caused by his war service, Ted Williams might have wiped out every batting record in the official files. He surely would have hit over .400 again in 1957, when his average was .388. But Ted was thirty-eight years old then (he in fact turned thirty-nine that August), and he missed many a hit just because his aging legs would no longer get him down to first base fast enough.

One of the major disappointments in Ted's life was his failure to play in more than a single World Series. The Red Sox, during his career, were destined to spend much of their time running after the Yankees for the pennant and hardly ever catching them. Boston, however, did win in 1946. But Ted's performance in the series against the Cardinals was severely affected by a bad elbow he received when he was hit by a pitch in a preseries exhibition game. (Manager Cronin or somebody upstairs had foolishly decided the exhibition would be a great way to keep the players in prime condition while waiting for the National League play-offs to end.) Ted simply could not swing as freely as he needed to in the championship contests, and his record at the plate was dismal. But he did have some fun in the third game, before a happy home crowd, when he took advantage of the "Williams shift" that put the Cards' third baseman over at second base when he stepped up to bat. Ted pushed a bunt down the third-base line, where there was no one to field it but the Saint Louis left fielder; Ted had the whole crowd yelling in glee as he pranced, with his enormous strides, down to first base. But Ted was woefully disappointed in himself during the series: frustrated and disgusted, he handed his full World Series check to Johnny Orlando, the clubhouse attendant.

Ted's heroics were instead reserved for the All-Star Games. His own choice of the greatest day in his career was the day he hit a home run to win the All-Star Game of 1941. But he also injured himself badly in one All-Star Game (in 1950) and almost ended his career. Trying to brace himself against the outfield wall with one elbow while catching a fly ball, he crashed hard into the concrete barrier. The impact chipped a bone badly and Ted needed surgery. Still, he came back to play nine more seasons and to lead the league in hitting twice more.

Because of the extremely loose rein Ted gave to his temper, he offered the Boston sportswriters many opportunities to picture him as a spoiled child, an insufferable egotist, and a disgrace to the game. He once screamed obscenities at a fan who hit him with a hot dog. He spat symbolically in the direction of the fans in every part of Fenway Park once when he was booed for dropping a fly ball (he was assessed — but he never paid — a $5000 fine for that). But there were always more fans in Boston who adored him than booed him. And the writers seemed mostly to be working out private grudges against Ted for his moodiness and his frequent failure to "cooperate" rather than criticizing his playing abilities.

When Ted performed one of his mighty deeds at Fenway Park (and he did win many a baseball game with a dramatic hit — sometimes a home run — that ended a game in victory), the fans would make the stands tremble with their ovation. Ted, in later years, expressed gratitude for all that support, but he refused to acknowledge applause in any way on the field. When he wound up his active career — in the most theatrical manner possible, by hitting a home run in his last time at bat — and the applause burst out like the roar of a naval battery, Ted did finally give in by tipping his cap to the standing crowd. But he stubbornly insisted that he had not really tipped his cap at all — just *removed* it.

By that time, however, Ted could not erase the many thoughtless statements he had made over the years (sometimes contradicting himself when his mood had changed); and he could not reasonably deny that he had often goofed off in a baseball game — forgetting, for instance, how many were out — or that he had sometimes sulked openly on the field. Still, there were many hearts in Boston that were solaced in his later years by Ted's wide-ranging humanitarianism and unfailing openhandedness. He devoted an unusual amount of time, uncomplainingly and without acclaim, to his pet charity, a fund to support cancer care and research. He even took pains to endorse personally all the *small* donation checks that were sent in, because he knew the two-dollar and five-dollar contributors — many of them youngsters — would especially value his autograph.

Ted grew rich in baseball, both from salaries and the income that his fame brought him through product endorsements. He may not have hurried home to his mother's fireside like the dutiful son when his labors were over, but he treated his family with generosity and kindness. He remained devoted to his friends — most of whom were unknown to the outside world and never could have passed as big shots — and he learned very early how to get along with girls. Still, he remained testy and given to bursts of sudden anger. He had no patience with untidiness (he had been raised surrounded by it) or with clumsiness.

Perhaps for that reason he failed to make a good manager. He accepted the job after long resisting the offers, but he found he could not make hitters out of players who did not devote themselves to the task as he had — batters who watched the ball game or the girls instead of the pitcher, who failed to learn any lessons when they went to the plate, who would not guard the plate when there were two strikes on them, who would try to cream a soft curve as if it were a fastball. Besides, by the time he left baseball as an active player, Ted's real passion was fishing — so he returned to it, after managing for four seasons, presumably without regrets.

Ted always wanted to be judged by his on-field accomplishments: his hitting records and his frequent dramatic contributions to victory. But there will always be some who prefer to remember his man-to-man generosity. And some will consider his finest moment not any single home run or game-winning hit, but the heartfelt speech he made when elected to the Hall of Fame. For on that occasion, instead of calling down blessings on the lords of baseball for honoring him, as was customary, Ted laid into them for failing to give due recognition to the many great black players who had been kept out of the major leagues for some sixty years by bigotry. Soon afterward, black heroes were listed on equal terms with Ted and all the white athletes enshrined in the Hall of Fame.